Better Homes and Gardens®

fresh and simple™

quick-
simmering
soups

Better Homes and Gardens® Books

Des Moines, Iowa

All of us at Better Homes and Gardens® Books
are dedicated to providing you with the information and ideas
you need to create delicious foods. We welcome your comments
and suggestions. Write to us at: Better Homes and Gardens®
Books, Cookbook Editorial Department, 1716 Locust St.,
Des Moines, IA 50309–3023.

If you would like to order additional copies of any of our books,
check with your local bookstore.

Our seal assures you that every recipe in
Quick-Simmering Soups has been tested in
the Better Homes and Gardens® Test
Kitchen. This means that each recipe is
practical and reliable, and meets our high
standards of taste appeal. We guarantee your
satisfaction with this book for as long as you
own it.

Better Homes and Gardens® Books
An imprint of Meredith® Books

Quick-Simmering Soups
Editor: Kristi M. Fuller
Writer: Margaret Agnew
Contributing Editors: Jennifer Darling, Jane Hemminger,
    Linda Henry, Nancy Hughes, Marty Schiel, Mary Williams,
    Spectrum Communication Services Inc.
Designer: Craig Hanken
Copy Chief: Catherine Hamrick
Copy and Production Editor: Terri Fredrickson
Contributing Copy Editor: Marcia Gilmer
Contributing Proofreaders: Gretchen Kauffmann, Susie Kling
Electronic Production Coordinator: Paula Forest
Editorial and Design Assistants: Judy Bailey, Treesa Landry,
    Karen Schirm
Test Kitchen Director: Sharon Stilwell
Test Kitchen Product Supervisors: Colleen Weeden and Jill Hoefler
Food Stylists: Karen Johnson
Photography: Jim Krantz, Kritsada Panichgul
Production Director: Douglas M. Johnston
Production Manager: Pam Kvitne
Assistant Prepress Manager: Marjorie J. Schenkelberg

Meredith® Books
Editor in Chief: James D. Blume
Design Director: Matt Strelecki
Managing Editor: Gregory H. Kayko
Executive Food Editor: Lisa Holderness
Director, Sales & Marketing, Retail: Michael A. Peterson
Director, Sales & Marketing, Special Markets: Rita McMullen
Director, Sales & Marketing, Home & Garden Center Channel:
    Ray Wolf
Director, Operations: George A. Susral

Vice President, General Manager: Jamie L. Martin

Better Homes and Gardens® Magazine
Editor in Chief: Jean LemMon
Executive Food Editor: Nancy Byal

Meredith Publishing Group
President, Publishing Group: Christopher M. Little
Vice President, Consumer Marketing
    & Development: Hal Oringer

Meredith Corporation
Chairman and Chief Executive Officer: William T. Kerr

Chairman of the Executive Committee: E. T. Meredith III

Pictured on front cover: Caribbean-Style Pork Stew
(see recipe, *page 32*)
Pictured on page 1: Pesto-Vegetable Soup
(see recipe, *page 85*)

contents

soups for the soul Simmer one of these heart-warming soups for your next family meal.   **6**

some like it hot Put a little sizzle into your soup bowl—chiles, spices, and heat prevail!   **28**

everyday gourmet Sophisticated but easy, these soups will inspire your creative side.   **44**

garden varieties Garden-fresh ingredients dominate these spectacular soups.   **58**

choice chowders Take your pick from the best variety of chowders around.   **72**

souper-quick simmers No time to fuss? This chapter has quick answers for dinnertime dilemma.   **84**

index   **94**

great bowls of soup!

Craving soup, but short on time? Doesn't matter. You can still enjoy a bowl of homemade soup in a snap—any day of the week, any time of the year.

Quick-Simmering Soups features 65 recipes that stir up fast. Choose from an array of light, warm-weather soups and hearty, cool-weather soups, including updated classics, ethnic favorites, chowders, and easy gourmet soups. This collection also helps you cut down on kitchen detail because most recipes require just one or two pans. Another bonus: Soup is often a meal in itself. Add a salad and warm, crusty bread—and soup's on!

soups for
the soul

allspice meatball stew

The exotic flavor of this hearty stew comes from the allspice berry of the pimiento tree. Allspice, which can be purchased whole or ground, gets its name because it tastes like a combination of cinnamon, nutmeg, and cloves.

Start to finish: 30 minutes   Makes 8 servings (10 cups)

In a Dutch oven combine the meatballs, green beans, carrots, beef broth, Worcestershire sauce, allspice, and cinnamon. Bring to boiling; reduce heat. Simmer, covered, for 10 minutes.

Stir in undrained tomatoes. Return to boiling; reduce heat. Simmer, covered, about 5 minutes more or until vegetables are crisp-tender.

Nutrition facts per serving: 233 cal., 13 g total fat (6 g sat. fat), 37 mg chol., 938 mg sodium, 18 g carbo., 4 g fiber, 12 g pro. Daily values: 86% vit. A, 22% vit. C, 5% calcium, 13% iron

Note: This soup freezes well. Freeze 1-, 2-, or 4-serving portions in sealed freezer containers. To reheat, place frozen soup in a large saucepan. Heat, covered, over medium heat about 30 minutes, stirring occasionally to break apart.

- 1 16-ounce package frozen prepared Italian-style meatballs
- 3 cups green beans cut into 2-inch pieces or frozen cut green beans
- 2 cups packaged peeled baby carrots
- 1 14½-ounce can beef broth
- 2 teaspoons Worcestershire sauce
- ½ to ¾ teaspoon ground allspice
- ½ teaspoon ground cinnamon
- 2 14½-ounce cans stewed tomatoes

easy cassoulet

The French know cassoulet as a classic, long-simmered dish consisting of white beans and various meats—sausages, pork, or goose. This version is a less time-consuming spin on the classic.

2 14½-ounce cans reduced-sodium chicken broth

2 stalks celery, chopped

2 medium carrots, chopped

1 large onion, chopped

3 cloves garlic, minced

2 teaspoons snipped fresh rosemary

2 15-ounce cans white kidney (cannellini) or navy beans, drained and rinsed

8 ounces cooked smoked turkey sausage links, halved lengthwise and sliced

1 cup chopped cooked chicken

½ cup dry white wine or reduced-sodium chicken broth

2 teaspoons snipped fresh thyme

Start to finish: 35 minutes   Makes 4 servings (7 cups)

In a large saucepan combine chicken broth, celery, carrots, onion, garlic, and rosemary. Bring to boiling; reduce heat. Simmer, uncovered, about 5 minutes or until vegetables are tender.

Stir in the beans, turkey sausage, chicken, wine, and thyme. Return to boiling; reduce heat. Simmer, covered, for 5 minutes more.

Nutrition facts per serving: 387 cal., 12 g total fat (3 g sat. fat), 70 mg chol., 1,335 mg sodium, 43 g carbo., 13 g fiber, 35 g pro. Daily values: 119% vit. A, 11% vit. C, 11% calcium, 29% iron

sausage & vegetable soup

Packaged shredded cabbage mix reduces the prep time and adds convenience for this hearty soup. Smoked sausage and sweet potato contribute new flavor dimensions.

Start to finish: 35 minutes   Makes 4 servings (6½ cups)

In a large saucepan cook sausage, onion, and celery over medium heat about 3 minutes or until vegetables are nearly tender. Stir in water, sweet potato, lima beans, pepper, and salt.

Bring to boiling; reduce heat. Simmer, covered, about 15 minutes or until vegetables are just tender. Stir in undrained tomatoes, cabbage mix, and basil. Return to boiling; reduce heat. Simmer, covered, for 2 minutes more.

Nutrition facts per serving: 215 cal., 7 g total fat (2 g sat. fat), 41 mg chol., 624 mg sodium, 28 g carbo., 7 g fiber, 14 g pro. Daily values: 110% vit. A, 75% vit. C, 9% calcium, 16% iron

- 8 **ounces cooked smoked turkey sausage links, halved lengthwise and sliced**
- 1 **medium onion, halved lengthwise and sliced**
- 1 **stalk celery, sliced**
- 3 **cups water**
- 1 **cup chopped peeled sweet potato**
- 1 **cup frozen lima beans**
- ¼ **teaspoon pepper**
- ⅛ **teaspoon salt**
- 1 **14½-ounce can tomatoes, cut up**
- 1½ **cups packaged shredded cabbage with carrot (cole slaw mix) or 1½ cups shredded cabbage**
- 2 **tablespoons snipped fresh basil**

pork & hominy stew

This savory combination could be described as a posole—a thick, hearty Mexican soup traditionally served as a main course at Christmas. Sprinkle shredded radishes over the top for a festive presentation.

12 ounces boneless pork strips for stir-frying

1 large onion, chopped

2 cloves garlic, minced

1 tablespoon cooking oil

4 cups chicken broth

2 medium carrots, thinly sliced

¼ teaspoon ground cumin

¼ teaspoon crushed red pepper

1 14½-ounce can hominy, drained

3 tablespoons snipped fresh cilantro

¼ cup shredded radishes

Start to finish: 30 minutes   Makes 4 servings (6 cups)

In a large saucepan cook pork, onion, and garlic in hot oil until pork is slightly pink in center. Remove pork mixture from saucepan; set aside. Add chicken broth, carrots, cumin, and pepper to saucepan.

Bring to boiling; reduce heat. Simmer, covered, about 8 minutes or until carrots are just tender. Add hominy, cilantro, and pork mixture; cook and stir until heated through. Top each serving with radishes.

Nutrition facts per serving: 290 cal., 12 g total fat (3 g sat. fat), 39 mg chol., 1,056 mg sodium, 26 g carbo., 3 g fiber, 20 g pro. Daily values: 118% vit. A, 8% vit. C, 4% calcium, 15% iron

moroccan lamb tagine

Lamb's richness pairs well with both spices and fruits, particularly the gingerroot, apples, and raisins called for here. If you have saffron on hand, add it for extra flavor and a brighter color. Serve this comforting soup with basmati or wild rice.

Start to finish: 35 minutes Makes 4 servings (7 cups)

In a large saucepan cook ground lamb, onion, and garlic until lamb is no longer pink. Drain well. Stir in the water, chicken broth, cilantro, gingerroot, pepper, paprika, and, if desired, saffron. Bring to boiling; reduce heat. Simmer, covered, for 10 minutes.

Stir in the apples or pears and raisins or dates. Return to boiling; reduce heat. Simmer, uncovered, for 1 to 2 minutes more or until apples are just slightly softened.

Nutrition facts per serving: 261 cal., 12 g total fat (5 g sat. fat), 57 mg chol., 381 mg sodium, 20 g carbo., 2 g fiber, 18 g pro. Daily values: 1% vit. A, 10% vit. C, 3% calcium, 11% iron

12 ounces lean ground lamb

 1 large onion, chopped

 3 cloves garlic, minced

 2 cups water

 1 14½-ounce can chicken broth

 ½ cup snipped fresh cilantro

 1 tablespoon grated gingerroot

 ¼ teaspoon pepper

 ¼ teaspoon paprika

 ⅛ teaspoon thread saffron, crushed, or dash ground saffron (optional)

 2 medium apples or pears, cored and thinly sliced

 ¼ cup raisins or snipped pitted dates

saffron

The spice called saffron comes from the stigmas or threadlike filaments of the purple crocus flower. Each flower contains only three stigmas, which are hand-picked and dried. It takes over 14,000 stigmas to provide an ounce of saffron. Because of the labor intensive process of harvesting the stigmas, saffron is very expensive. You only need a small amount to flavor your recipes, though—a little will go a long way. Saffron comes in thin threads. To release the flavor, crush the threads by rubbing them between your fingers.

greek minestrone

Arborio rice is an Italian-grown grain that is shorter and plumper than any other short-grain rice. Traditionally used to make creamy risotto, it adds a similar texture to this bean and vegetable soup.

2 stalks celery, finely chopped

1 large onion, finely chopped

2 cloves garlic, minced

1 tablespoon olive oil

5 cups beef broth

1 cup water

½ cup uncooked Arborio rice

6 cups torn spinach

1 15-ounce can great northern beans, drained and rinsed

3 medium tomatoes, chopped (about 2 cups)

1 medium zucchini, coarsely chopped (about 1½ cups)

¼ cup snipped fresh thyme

¼ teaspoon cracked black pepper

½ cup crumbled feta cheese (2 ounces)

Start to finish: 40 minutes   Makes 6 servings (10½ cups)

In a Dutch oven cook celery, onion, and garlic in hot oil until tender. Add beef broth, water, and rice. Bring to boiling; reduce heat. Simmer, covered, for 15 minutes.

Add the torn spinach, beans, tomatoes, zucchini, thyme, and pepper. Cook and stir until heated through. Top each serving with feta cheese.

Nutrition facts per serving: 252 cal., 6 g total fat (2 g sat. fat), 8 mg chol., 834 mg sodium, 39 g carbo., 8 g fiber, 13 g pro. Daily values: 44% vit. A, 58% vit. C, 15% calcium, 31% iron

the **best** broths

When a recipe calls for chicken, beef, or vegetable broth, you can use a homemade stock recipe or substitute commercially canned broth. Just remember that the canned varieties usually are saltier than homemade stocks, so hold off on adding extra salt until the end of cooking. Then, season to taste. Another option is to try a canned reduced-sodium broth. Bouillon cubes and granules diluted according to package directions may be used, but they are also saltier than homemade stocks.

chunky ratatouille stew

Simmer the pleasures of a summer garden into this stew. Like typical ratatouille, it combines eggplant, tomatoes, onion, green sweet pepper, and green beans or zucchini. For a fun presentation, serve in hollowed eggplant halves.

Start to finish: 35 minutes   Makes 4 servings (6 cups)

In a Dutch oven cook the onion and green pepper in hot oil until tender. Stir in the mushrooms, eggplant, and green beans. Add beef broth and wine.

Bring to boiling; reduce heat. Simmer, covered, for 8 to 10 minutes or until vegetables are tender. Stir in undrained tomatoes and basil; heat through. Sprinkle each serving with provolone cheese.

Nutrition facts per serving: 163 cal., 8 g total fat (3 g sat. fat), 10 mg chol., 955 mg sodium, 16 g carbo., 3 g fiber, 8 g pro. Daily values: 13% vit. A, 65% vit. C, 14% calcium, 10% iron

- 1 large onion, chopped
- 1 cup chopped green sweet pepper
- 1 tablespoon olive oil
- 2 cups small whole fresh mushrooms (about 6 ounces), stems removed
- 2 cups peeled and chopped eggplant (about 6 ounces)
- 4 ounces green beans, cut into 1-inch pieces, or 1 small zucchini, thinly sliced (about 1 cup)
- 2 cups beef broth
- 2 tablespoons dry red wine
- 1 14½-ounce can diced tomatoes with roasted garlic and red pepper
- 1 tablespoon snipped fresh basil
- ½ cup shredded provolone cheese (2 ounces)

wild rice, barley, & mushroom soup

It's hard to resist this enticing soup. The nutty flavor and chewy texture of wild rice and barley make pleasant contrasts to the earthy flavor and soft texture of the mushrooms. Add a splash of Madeira for a sophisticated accent.

16

1 cup water

¼ cup quick-cooking barley

3 medium leeks, washed, trimmed, and thinly sliced

1 medium carrot, sliced

1 small parsnip, finely chopped

1 clove garlic, minced

1 tablespoon margarine or butter

3 cups sliced fresh mushrooms (about 8 ounces)

1 tablespoon snipped fresh sage or 1 teaspoon dried sage, crushed

2½ cups vegetable broth

¾ cup cooked wild rice

2 tablespoons Madeira wine or dry sherry (optional)

Salt

Pepper

Start to finish: 25 minutes   Makes 3 servings (5 cups)

In a small saucepan combine water and barley. Bring mixture to boiling; reduce heat. Simmer, covered, for 10 minutes.

Meanwhile, in a large saucepan cook leeks, carrot, parsnip, and garlic in hot margarine or butter for 5 minutes. Stir in the mushrooms and dried sage (if using). Cook 5 to 10 minutes more or just until mushrooms are tender. Stir in the vegetable broth, cooked wild rice, and, if desired, Madeira. If using, stir in fresh sage. Cook and stir until heated through. Season to taste with salt and pepper.

Nutrition facts per serving: 223 cal., 6 g total fat (1 g sat. fat), 0 mg chol., 854 mg sodium, 45 g carbo., 9 g fiber, 7 g pro. Daily values: 60% vit. A, 20% vit. C, 5% calcium, 24% iron

mushroom know-how
Store fresh mushrooms in the refrigerator. Instead of an airtight container, use a cotton bag or a brown paper sack that will let them breathe. Avoid soaking or washing mushrooms prior to storage; they will absorb water and deteriorate more quickly. Just before using the mushrooms, clean them by wiping with a damp cloth or paper towel.

potato soup
with blue cheese

The happy marriage of potatoes and blue cheese makes for an idyllic wintry soup. The potatoes promise creamy texture; the cheese pledges robust flavor. Added just before serving, vibrant tomato lends color and freshness.

Start to finish: 35 minutes   Makes 3 servings (4 cups)

In a medium saucepan combine potatoes, water, onion, bouillon granules, and pepper. Bring to boiling; reduce heat. Simmer, covered, about 20 minutes or until potatoes are tender. Mash potatoes slightly; do not drain.

Meanwhile, in a screw-top jar combine ½ cup of the milk and the flour; cover and shake well. Add to saucepan; add the remaining milk. Cook and stir until thickened and bubbly. Cook and stir for 1 minute more.

Add the blue cheese and parsley; stir until the cheese melts. Top each serving with tomato and green onion.

Nutrition facts per serving: 289 cal., 7 g total fat (4 g sat. fat), 21 mg chol., 829 mg sodium, 46 g carbo., 3 g fiber, 12 g pro. Daily values: 15% vit. A, 36% vit. C, 23% calcium, 8% iron

3 medium potatoes, peeled and chopped (about 2 cups)

1 cup water

1 small onion, chopped

2 teaspoons instant chicken bouillon granules

⅛ teaspoon pepper

2 cups milk

2 tablespoons all-purpose flour

¼ cup crumbled blue cheese (1 ounce)

2 tablespoons snipped fresh parsley

½ cup finely chopped tomato

2 tablespoons thinly sliced green onion

curried lentil soup

Humble lentils step out in spicy style with a flavor kick of gingerroot, curry powder, cumin, and cilantro. If you like, a spoonful of sour cream swirled into the soup adds a complementary richness.

- 6 cups reduced-sodium chicken broth
- 1½ cups thinly sliced green onions
- 2 medium carrots, chopped
- 1 cup dried brown lentils, drained and rinsed
- 1 tablespoon grated gingerroot
- 1 teaspoon curry powder
- 1 teaspoon ground cumin
- ⅛ to ¼ teaspoon ground red pepper
- ¼ cup snipped fresh cilantro
- ½ cup dairy sour cream (optional)

  Fresh cilantro sprigs or green onions (optional)

Start to finish: 40 minutes   Makes 4 servings (6 cups)

In a large saucepan combine the chicken broth, green onions, carrots, lentils, gingerroot, curry powder, cumin, and red pepper. Bring mixture to boiling; reduce heat. Simmer, covered, for 25 to 30 minutes or until lentils are tender.

Stir in the snipped cilantro; cook for 1 minute more. If desired, top each serving with sour cream and garnish with cilantro sprigs.

Nutrition facts per serving: 201 cal., 3 g total fat (0 g sat. fat), 0 mg chol., 986 mg sodium, 32 g carbo., 3 g fiber, 15 g pro. Daily values: 88% vit. A, 16% vit. C, 4% calcium, 36% iron

asparagus & cheese
potato soup

A treasure of spring—tender, purple-tinged asparagus—is featured in this soup. Sour cream lends a tangy flavor to this creamy delight.

Start to finish: 35 minutes   Makes 4 servings (5½ cups)

In a large saucepan cook onion in hot oil until tender. Sprinkle flour over onion and stir to coat. Add the asparagus, milk, chicken broth, potatoes, salt, and red pepper.

Cook and stir until thickened and bubbly; reduce heat. Simmer, covered, for 10 to 12 minutes or until vegetables are just tender, stirring occasionally. Add cheddar cheese, tomato, and sour cream; stir until cheese melts.

Nutrition facts per serving: 383 cal., 21 g total fat (11 g sat. fat), 48 mg chol., 730 mg sodium, 31 g carbo., 3 g fiber, 18 g pro. Daily values: 28% vit. A, 56% vit. C, 34% calcium, 15% iron

- 1 **large onion, chopped**
- 4 **teaspoons cooking oil**
- 3 **tablespoons all-purpose flour**
- 2 **cups 1-inch pieces asparagus spears or broccoli flowerets**
- 2 **cups milk**
- 1 **14½-ounce can chicken broth**
- 8 **ounces red potatoes, cubed (about 1½ cups)**
- ¼ **teaspoon salt**
- ⅛ **teaspoon ground red pepper**
- 1 **cup shredded sharp cheddar cheese (4 ounces)**
- 1 **small tomato, seeded and chopped**
- ⅓ **cup dairy sour cream**

black & white bean chili

Calling all hearty appetites! This satisfying blend of black beans, white kidney beans, jicama, and chile peppers boasts a pronounced south-of-the-border flavor.

1 medium onion, chopped

1 clove garlic, minced

1 tablespoon cooking oil

1 15-ounce can white kidney (cannellini) beans, drained and rinsed

1 15-ounce can black beans, drained and rinsed

1 14½-ounce can chicken broth

1 cup chopped peeled jicama or potato

1 4-ounce can diced green chile peppers

1 teaspoon ground cumin

2 tablespoons snipped fresh cilantro

1 tablespoon lime juice

¼ cup crumbled queso fresco or feta cheese (1 ounce)

Start to finish: 35 minutes   Makes 4 servings (5 cups)

In a large saucepan cook onion and garlic in hot oil until tender. Stir in white kidney beans, black beans, chicken broth, jicama or potato, chile peppers, and cumin.

Bring to boiling; reduce heat. Simmer, covered, about 10 minutes or until jicama is crisp-tender or potato is tender. Stir in cilantro and lime juice; heat through. Top each serving with queso fresco or feta cheese.

Nutrition facts per serving: 254 cal., 9 g total fat (3 g sat. fat), 15 mg chol., 1,012 mg sodium, 37 g carbo., 10 g fiber, 19 g pro. Daily values: 2% vit. A, 32% vit. C, 16% calcium, 24% iron

the **mexican** potato

Jicama is often referred to as the Mexican potato. This large, bulbous root vegetable has a thin brown skin and white crunchy flesh. Unlike regular potatoes, jicama has a sweet, nutty flavor and is good both raw and cooked. It is available from November through May and can be purchased in Mexican markets and most large supermarkets. Jicama will last up to 5 days stored in the refrigerator. The thin skin should be peeled just before using. When cooked, jicama retains its crisp, water chestnut-type texture.

bayou shrimp soup

Enjoy the flavor of gumbo without all the fuss. This stew incorporates familiar gumbo ingredients—rice, tomatoes, sausage, and shrimp—minus the long cooking time.

Start to finish: 35 minutes   Makes 4 servings (6½ cups)

In a large saucepan cook the sausage, sweet pepper, and onion over medium-high heat for 6 to 7 minutes or until vegetables are tender, stirring frequently. Add chicken broth, steak sauce, and, if using, dried thyme. If not using andouille sausage, add the crushed red pepper.

Bring to boiling; reduce heat. Simmer, covered, for 10 minutes.

Add the shrimp, tomatoes, cooked rice, and, if using, fresh thyme. Cook and stir until heated through.

Nutrition facts per serving: 404 cal., 20 g total fat (7 g sat. fat), 149 mg chol., 1,345 mg sodium, 27 g carbo., 2 g fiber, 28 g pro. Daily values: 12% vit. A, 62% vit. C, 5% calcium, 27% iron

8 ounces cooked andouille or other smoked sausage links, thinly sliced

1 medium green sweet pepper, chopped

1 medium onion, chopped

1 14½-ounce can reduced-sodium chicken broth

1 tablespoon steak sauce

2 tablespoons snipped fresh thyme or 1½ teaspoons dried thyme, crushed

¼ teaspoon crushed red pepper (optional)

8 ounces frozen, peeled, cooked shrimp

2 cups chopped tomatoes

1½ cups cooked rice

shrimp & greens soup

Although great any time of year, this fresh-tasting seafood soup is light enough to serve during the summer. The savory combination of shrimp, shredded bok choy, and leek is embellished with an accent of lemon pepper.

Start to finish: 30 minutes   Makes 4 servings (7 cups)

Thaw shrimp, if frozen.

In a large saucepan cook leek and garlic in hot oil over medium-high heat about 2 minutes or until leek is tender. Carefully add chicken broth, parsley, marjoram, and lemon-pepper seasoning. Bring to boiling; add shrimp. Return to boiling; reduce heat.

Simmer, uncovered, for 2 minutes. Stir in the bok choy. Cook about 1 minute more or until the shrimp turn pink.

Nutrition facts per serving: 147 cal., 6 g total fat (1 g sat. fat), 131 mg chol., 1,093 mg sodium, 5 g carbo., 2 g fiber, 18 g pro. Daily values: 10% vit. A, 25% vit. C, 6% calcium, 18% iron

12 ounces peeled and deveined fresh or frozen shrimp

1 large leek, sliced

2 cloves garlic, minced

1 tablespoon olive oil

3 14½-ounce cans reduced-sodium chicken broth or vegetable broth

1 tablespoon snipped fresh Italian flat-leaf parsley or parsley

1 tablespoon snipped fresh marjoram or thyme

¼ teaspoon lemon-pepper seasoning

2 cups shredded bok choy or spinach leaves

creamy chicken
vegetable soup

Longing for a simpler way to cook? Quick-cooking rice and purchased alfredo sauce save time and effort in a soup that tastes like it took hours to prepare.

3 cups chicken broth

2 medium carrots, thinly sliced

2 stalks celery, thinly sliced

1 cup chopped cooked chicken

1 small zucchini, thinly sliced (about 1 cup)

½ cup uncooked quick-cooking rice

1 10-ounce container refrigerated light alfredo sauce

¼ cup chopped roasted red sweet peppers or one 4-ounce jar diced pimentos, drained

1 tablespoon snipped fresh thyme

Start to finish: 30 minutes   Makes 4 servings (6 cups)

In a Dutch oven combine chicken broth, carrots, and celery. Bring to boiling; reduce heat. Simmer, covered, for 10 minutes.

Stir in chicken, zucchini, and rice. Remove from heat and let stand, covered, about 5 minutes or until rice is tender. Stir in alfredo sauce, roasted red peppers, and thyme. Return to heat; heat through.

Nutrition facts per serving: 349 cal., 14 g total fat (7 g sat. fat), 65 mg chol., 1,286 mg sodium, 34 g carbo., 2 g fiber, 22 g pro. Daily values: 99% vit. A, 49% vit. C, 16% calcium, 12% iron

cooked **chicken** choices

When a recipe calls for cooked chicken, you can use a package of frozen chopped cooked chicken. Or, purchase a deli-roasted chicken. A cooked whole chicken will yield 1½ to 2 cups boneless chopped meat. If you have more time, you can poach chicken breasts. For 2 cups cubed cooked chicken, in a large skillet place 12 ounces skinless, boneless chicken breasts and 1½ cups water. Bring to boiling; reduce heat. Cover and simmer for 12 to 14 minutes or until chicken is tender and no longer pink. Drain chicken well and cut up. Add to the soup and cook just long enough to heat through.

chicken & rice soup with dumplings

This soul-warming soup will remind you of your grandmother's old-fashioned chicken and dumplings. The heat from the boiling soup helps cook the dumplings to a light, tender perfection.

Start to finish: 35 minutes   Makes 4 or 5 servings (8 cups)

In a large saucepan cook mushrooms, celery, and carrot in 1 tablespoon hot margarine until tender. Carefully stir in chicken broth, chicken, peas, rice, thyme, and pepper. Bring to boiling.

Meanwhile, prepare dumplings. Drop dumpling batter from a small spoon to make 16 mounds on top of the boiling soup; reduce heat. Simmer, covered, about 10 minutes or until dumplings are cooked.

Dumplings: In a small bowl beat together 2 eggs, ¼ cup melted margarine or butter, and ¼ teaspoon salt. Stir in ⅔ cup instant flour (Wondra) or all-purpose flour.

Nutrition facts per serving: 491 cal., 28 g total fat (1 g sat. fat), 183 mg chol., 1,222 mg sodium, 37 g carbo., 3 g fiber, 33 g pro. Daily values: 83% vit. A, 11% vit. C, 5% calcium, 27% iron

1   cup sliced fresh mushrooms

1   stalk celery, sliced

1   medium carrot, chopped

1   tablespoon margarine or butter

5   cups reduced-sodium
      chicken broth

2   cups chopped cooked chicken

1   cup frozen peas

½   cup uncooked quick-cooking rice

2   teaspoons snipped fresh thyme or
      1 teaspoon dried thyme, crushed

¼   teaspoon pepper

1   recipe Dumplings

some like it hot

gingered pork & cabbage soup

Asian cooks have long known that the peppery, slightly sweet taste of gingerroot perfectly matches mild-flavored pork. Here, the combination is even better joined with a bit of fresh mint.

Start to finish: 40 minutes   Makes 6 servings (10 cups)

In a medium saucepan bring the 6 cups broth to boiling. Meanwhile, trim fat from pork. Cut pork into ½-inch cubes. In a large saucepan cook pork, onion, garlic, and gingerroot in hot oil until pork is brown.

Add vegetable broth. Bring to boiling. Stir in tomatoes and carrots. Return to boiling; reduce heat. Simmer, covered, for 15 minutes.

Stir in the pasta and cook for 6 to 8 minutes more or until pasta is tender but still firm. Stir in sliced Chinese cabbage and mint. If desired, garnish with Chinese cabbage leaves.

Nutrition facts per serving: 141 cal., 6 g total fat (1 g sat. fat), 16 mg chol., 961 mg sodium, 21 g carbo., 2 g fiber, 8 g pro. Daily values: 65% vit. A, 47% vit. C, 5% calcium, 14% iron

6	cups vegetable broth or chicken broth
8	ounces boneless pork sirloin, cut ½ inch thick
1	large onion, chopped
4	cloves garlic, minced
2	teaspoons grated gingerroot
1	tablespoon cooking oil
3	small tomatoes, chopped
2	medium carrots, finely chopped
½	cup dried anelli pasta
4	cups thinly sliced Chinese cabbage
¼	cup snipped fresh mint
	Chinese cabbage leaves (optional)

vegetable broth business

When a recipe calls for vegetable broth, you can use canned broth or bouillon cubes, or prepare a homemade stock. An easy way to make your own vegetable stock is to save the water in which vegetables are boiled and freeze it in a covered container. Keep saving the liquid from the vegetables you prepare, and in the course of time you will have a basic vegetable stock that's ready to use.

chinese glass noodle soup

Tender strips of pork, broccoli, and bean threads comprise the main ingredients in this broth-based soup. Crushed red pepper, gingerroot, and toasted sesame oil supply the prominent Asian flavor.

2 ounces bean threads
(cellophane noodles)

2 cloves garlic, minced

1 tablespoon grated gingerroot

2 tablespoons cooking oil

3 cups broccoli flowerets

12 ounces lean boneless pork,
cut into bite-size strips

3 14½-ounce cans reduced-sodium
chicken broth

1 teaspoon crushed red pepper

1 teaspoon toasted sesame oil

Start to finish: 30 minutes   Makes 4 servings (8 cups)

Place bean threads in a bowl; pour enough boiling water over bean threads to cover. Let stand for 10 minutes; drain. Use scissors to cut bean threads into 2-inch lengths; set aside.

Meanwhile, in a large saucepan cook the garlic and gingerroot in 1 tablespoon hot cooking oil over medium heat for 15 seconds. Add the broccoli. Cover and cook for 3 to 4 minutes or until crisp-tender, stirring once or twice. Remove mixture from saucepan; set aside.

Add remaining cooking oil to saucepan. Add the pork; cook and stir for 2 to 3 minutes or until slightly pink in center. Carefully add chicken broth, red pepper, and sesame oil. Bring to boiling; reduce heat. Stir in bean threads and vegetable mixture; heat through.

Nutrition facts per serving: 283 cal., 15 g total fat (3 g sat. fat), 38 mg chol., 989 mg sodium, 18 g carbo., 2 g fiber, 18 g pro. Daily values: 7% vit. A, 54% vit. C, 2% calcium, 7% iron

garlic, black bean, & sausage soup

Cuban flavors dominate this black bean soup, which features a hearty combination of sausage, tomatoes, and fennel seed. A spoonful of sour cream tops each serving.

Start to finish: 40 minutes   Makes 4 or 5 servings (6 cups)

In a large saucepan cook sausage, onion, garlic, and fennel seed over medium-high heat for 10 to 12 minutes or until sausage is no longer pink. Drain well.

Stir in the black beans and beef broth. Bring to boiling; reduce heat. Simmer, covered, for 15 minutes.

Meanwhile, if desired, stir the red pepper into the sour cream. Cover and refrigerate until ready to serve.

Just before serving, stir the tomatoes and oregano into soup; heat through.* Top each serving with sour cream mixture.

Nutrition facts per serving: 429 cal., 20 g total fat (8 g sat. fat), 55 mg chol., 1,453 mg sodium, 42 g carbo., 12 g fiber, 30 g pro. Daily values: 10% vit. A, 44% vit. C, 11% calcium, 27% iron

Note: If a thinner consistency is desired, add a small amount of water.

- 12 ounces bulk mild Italian sausage
- 1½ cups chopped onion
- 10 cloves garlic, minced
- ½ teaspoon fennel seed, crushed
- 2 15-ounce cans black beans, drained and rinsed
- 1 14½-ounce can beef broth
  Dash ground red pepper (optional)
- ¼ cup dairy sour cream
- 2 cups chopped tomatoes
- 2 tablespoons snipped fresh oregano

caribbean-style pork stew

The flavor of a plantain will depend on the ripeness. A ripe, black-skinned plantain tastes like a banana. An almost-ripe, yellow plantain tastes similar to sweet potatoes. Unripe, green plantains taste starchy but lose the starchy flavor upon cooking.

1   15-ounce can black beans, drained and rinsed

1   14½-ounce can beef broth

1¾ cups water

12 ounces cooked lean boneless pork, cut into bite-size strips

3   plantains, peeled and cubed

1   cup chopped tomatoes

½ of a 16-ounce package (2 cups) frozen pepper stir-fry vegetables (such as yellow, green, and red sweet peppers and onion)

1   tablespoon grated gingerroot

1   teaspoon ground cumin

¼ teaspoon crushed red pepper

¼ teaspoon salt

3   cups hot cooked rice

    Crushed red pepper (optional)

    Fresh pineapple slices (optional)

Start to finish: 30 minutes   Makes 6 servings (8½ cups)

In a Dutch oven combine the beans, broth, and water; heat to boiling.

Add the pork, plantains, and tomatoes to the bean mixture. Stir in the frozen vegetables, gingerroot, cumin, the ¼ teaspoon red pepper, and the salt. Return mixture to boiling; reduce heat and simmer, covered, for 10 minutes or until plantains are tender. Serve with hot rice. If desired, sprinkle with additional crushed red pepper and garnish with pineapple.

Nutrition facts per serving: 425 cal., 9 g total fat (3 g sat. fat), 52 mg chol., 547 mg sodium, 66 carbo., 6 g fiber, 26 g pro. Daily values: 44% vit. A, 62% vit. C, 5% calcium, 4% iron

yucatan soup with lime

The bright flavors of the Yucatan dance in your mouth as you sip this highly spiced soup. The addition of lime juice provides a tangy surprise.

12 ounces skinless, boneless chicken breasts, cut into bite-size pieces

3 cloves garlic, minced

1 tablespoon olive oil or cooking oil

1 tablespoon hot chili powder

½ teaspoon cumin seed, crushed, or ¼ teaspoon ground cumin

¼ to ½ teaspoon crushed red pepper (optional)

2 14½-ounce cans chicken broth

½ cup chopped green onions

1 large tomato, chopped

3 tablespoons lime juice

Start to finish: 30 minutes   Makes 4 servings (5½ cups)

In a Dutch oven cook the chicken and garlic in hot oil over medium-high heat until chicken is no longer pink. Stir in chili powder, cumin, and, if desired, crushed red pepper. Cook and stir for 30 seconds. Stir in the chicken broth and green onions.

Bring to boiling; reduce heat. Simmer, uncovered, for 10 minutes. Remove from heat. Stir in the tomato and lime juice.

Nutrition facts per serving: 178 cal., 8 g total fat (1 g sat. fat), 45 mg chol., 719 mg sodium, 6 g carbo., 1 g fiber, 21 g pro. Daily values: 12% vit. A, 25% vit. C, 2% calcium, 12% iron

pork, corn, & three-pepper soup

Experience a peck of peppers in this soup. There are actually three different types of peppers in this corn-filled soup: red sweet pepper, green chile peppers, and hot ground red pepper. Adjust the heat level by adding more or less ground red pepper.

Start to finish: 30 minutes   Makes 4 servings (5½ cups)

In a large saucepan cook pork in hot oil for 2 to 3 minutes or until slightly pink in center. Remove from pan; cover and keep warm. Add red sweet pepper and onion to saucepan and cook until tender.

Stir in the cream-style corn, chicken broth, milk, frozen corn, and undrained chile peppers. Bring to boiling; reduce heat. Simmer, covered, for 5 minutes.

Stir in pork, parsley, salt, and ground red pepper; heat through.

Nutrition facts per serving: 281 cal., 12 g total fat (3 g sat. fat), 43 mg chol., 768 mg sodium, 30 g carbo., 2 g fiber, 19 g pro. Daily values: 18% vit. A, 73% vit. C, 10% calcium, 10% iron

- 12 **ounces lean boneless pork, cut into bite-size strips**
- 1 **tablespoon cooking oil**
- ½ **cup chopped red sweet pepper**
- 1 **small onion, chopped**
- 1 **14¾-ounce can cream-style corn**
- 1 **cup chicken broth**
- 1 **cup milk**
- ½ **cup frozen whole kernel corn**
- 1 **4-ounce can diced green chile peppers**
- ¼ **cup snipped fresh parsley**
- ¼ **teaspoon salt**
- ¼ **teaspoon ground red pepper**

chicken chili with rice

Tomatillos often are referred to as Mexican green tomatoes because they resemble a small green tomato and are often used in Mexican cooking. They hint of a lemon and apple flavor. Tomatillos add a unique taste to salads, salsas, and this chunky soup.

Start to finish: 35 minutes   Makes 4 servings (5 cups)

In a large saucepan cook the garlic and jalapeño pepper in hot oil for 30 seconds. Carefully stir in onions, chicken broth, chili powder, cumin, oregano, salt, white pepper, and red pepper.

Bring to boiling; reduce heat. Simmer, covered, for 20 minutes. Add beans, chicken, and tomatillos; cook and stir until heated through. Serve over rice.

Nutrition facts per serving: 335 cal., 8 g total fat (1 g sat. fat), 34 mg chol., 417 mg sodium, 51 g carbo., 8 g fiber, 23 g pro. Daily values: 6% vit. A, 23% vit. C, 6% calcium, 26% iron

3 cloves garlic, minced

1 fresh jalapeño pepper, seeded
   and finely chopped

1 tablespoon cooking oil

2 cups frozen small whole onions

1 cup reduced-sodium chicken
   broth or chicken broth

2 teaspoons chili powder

1 teaspoon ground cumin

1 teaspoon dried oregano, crushed

¼ teaspoon salt

⅛ teaspoon ground white pepper

⅛ teaspoon ground red pepper

1 19-ounce can white kidney
   (cannellini) beans,
   drained and rinsed

1 cup chopped cooked chicken

1 cup chopped tomatillos

2 cups hot cooked rice or couscous

chipotle chile pepper soup

If you have never tried chipotle (chih-POHT-lay) peppers, jalapeño peppers that have been smoked, here's your chance. As well as adding the heat, these peppers add a pleasant smoked flavor.

- **1 large onion, finely chopped**
- **4 cloves garlic, minced**
- **1 tablespoon olive oil or cooking oil**
- **12 ounces skinless, boneless chicken breasts, cut into bite-size pieces**
- **1 14½-ounce can chicken broth**
- **2 teaspoons chopped canned chipotle peppers in adobo sauce**
- **½ teaspoon sugar**
- **¼ teaspoon salt**
- **2 cups chopped tomatoes or one 14½-ounce can low-sodium diced tomatoes**
- **¼ cup snipped fresh cilantro**

Start to finish: 35 minutes   Makes 3 servings (4 cups)

In a Dutch oven cook the onion and garlic in hot oil over medium-high heat about 4 minutes or until tender. Add the chicken; cook for 2 minutes. Stir in the chicken broth, chipotle peppers, sugar, and salt.

Bring to boiling; reduce heat. Simmer, uncovered, for 15 minutes. Remove from heat. Stir in the tomatoes and the snipped cilantro.

Nutrition facts per serving: 246 cal., 9 g total fat (2 g sat. fat), 60 mg chol., 735 mg sodium, 14 g carbo., 3 g fiber, 26 g pro. Daily values: 16% vit. A, 53% vit. C, 3% calcium, 13% iron

Note: The sugar cuts the sharpness of the tomatoes, giving a mellow, rich flavor to the soup without adding noticeable sweetness.

finishing **touches**
Keep the soup garnishes simple. A sprinkling of snipped fresh herbs or sliced green onions adds nice color to any soup, while croutons offer a little crunch. A slice of lemon, a little grated cheese, a few chopped nuts, sieved cooked egg white or yolk, or shredded radishes add complementary color to many soups.

mushroom tortelloni in curry cream

Indonesian in flavor, this quick-cooking soup captures your attention with its wonderful aroma. Curry, coconut, and basil all add to the allure. If you're unable to find tortelloni, a larger version of tortellini, use tortellini instead.

40

1 shallot, finely chopped

1 fresh jalapeño pepper, seeded and finely chopped

1 clove garlic, minced

2 teaspoons curry powder

1 tablespoon cooking oil

1 14½-ounce can chicken broth

1 14-ounce can unsweetened coconut milk

1 9-ounce package refrigerated mushroom tortelloni

1 tablespoon snipped fresh basil

1 medium tomato, chopped

Chopped peanuts (optional)

Start to finish: 30 minutes   Makes 4 servings (5 cups)

In a medium saucepan cook shallot, jalapeño pepper, garlic, and curry powder in hot oil about 1 minute or until shallot is tender. Stir in chicken broth. Bring to boiling; reduce heat. Simmer, covered, for 5 minutes.

Stir in the coconut milk, tortelloni, and basil. Cook and stir about 5 minutes more or until pasta is tender but still firm. Stir in the tomato. Cook and stir until heated through, but do not boil.

If desired, garnish each serving with peanuts.

Nutrition facts per serving: 306 cal., 14 g total fat (7 g sat. fat), 24 mg chol., 649 mg sodium, 35 g carbo., 3 g fiber, 10 g pro. Daily values: 8% vit. A, 20% vit. C, 9% calcium, 18% iron

thai red curry soup with shrimp

Red curry paste, an essential ingredient in Thai cooking, imparts spiciness to this soup. Coconut milk, often called for in curry dishes, can be purchased in cans at Asian markets and some supermarkets.

1 tablespoon cooking oil

12 ounces peeled and deveined fresh shrimp, halved lengthwise

1 tablespoon red curry paste

1 14½-ounce can chicken broth

1 tablespoon fish sauce (optional)

8 ounces green beans, trimmed and cut into bite-size pieces, or one 9-ounce package frozen cut green beans, thawed

1 cup unsweetened coconut milk

2 tablespoons snipped fresh basil

Start to finish: 25 minutes   Makes 4 servings (5 cups)

Pour cooking oil into a large saucepan; preheat over medium-high heat. Stir-fry shrimp and curry paste in hot oil for 2 to 3 minutes or until shrimp turn pink. Remove shrimp from saucepan; set aside.

In same saucepan bring the chicken broth and, if desired, fish sauce to boiling. Add the green beans. Return to boiling; reduce heat.

Simmer, uncovered, about 5 minutes or until beans are crisp-tender. Stir in shrimp and coconut milk; heat through. Stir in basil.

Nutrition facts per serving: 249 cal., 16 g total fat (11 g sat. fat), 131 mg chol., 656 mg sodium, 8 g carbo., 2 g fiber, 19 g pro. Daily values: 9% vit. A, 11% vit. C, 5% calcium, 24% iron

selecting shrimp

Shrimp are sold by the pound. The price per pound usually is determined by the size of the shrimp—the bigger the shrimp, the higher the price and the fewer per pound. Fresh shrimp should be moist and firm, have translucent flesh, and smell fresh. Signs of poor quality are an ammonia smell and blackened edges or spots on the shells.

cajun fish soup

This tongue-tingling soup gets its spirited flavor from Cajun seasoning, a blend of ingredients such as garlic, chiles, black pepper, and mustard. Depending on the brand of seasoning you buy, however, the combination of ingredients may vary.

Start to finish: 25 minutes   Makes 4 servings (7½ cups)

Thaw the fish or shrimp, if frozen. If using fish, cut into 1-inch pieces; set fish aside.

In a large saucepan or Dutch oven combine the vegetable or chicken broth, mushrooms, summer squash or zucchini, onion, garlic, and Cajun seasoning. Bring to boiling; reduce heat. Simmer, covered, for 5 minutes or until the vegetables are tender.

Stir in the fish or shrimp and undrained tomatoes. Bring just to boiling; reduce heat. Simmer, covered, for 2 to 3 minutes or until the fish flakes easily with a fork or the shrimp turn pink. Remove from heat. Stir in the oregano and lemon peel.

Nutrition facts per serving: 149 cal., 2 gm total fat (0 gm sat. fat), 40 mg chol., 608 mg sodium, 20 gm carbo., 5 gm fiber, 17 gm pro. Daily values: 18% vit. A, 32% vit. C, 4% calcium, 9% iron

12 ounces fresh or frozen fish fillets
     or peeled and deveined shrimp

1 14½-ounce can vegetable broth or
     chicken broth

1 cup sliced fresh mushrooms

1 small yellow summer squash or
     zucchini, halved lengthwise and
     sliced

½ cup chopped onion

1 clove garlic, minced

1 to 1½ teaspoons Cajun seasoning

2 14½-ounce cans reduced-sodium
     stewed tomatoes

2 tablespoons snipped fresh oregano

½ teaspoon finely shredded
     lemon peel

everyday
gourmet

asian chicken noodle soup

Chicken soup is known universally as a comforting cure-all for the body and soul. Soy sauce, gingerroot, and pea pods add an Asian flair to this version of a classic favorite.

Start to finish: 20 minutes   Makes 3 servings (5½ cups)

In a large saucepan combine chicken broth, water, noodles, soy sauce, gingerroot, and crushed red pepper. Bring to boiling. Stir in the sweet pepper, carrot, and green onions. Return to boiling; reduce heat. Simmer, covered, for 4 to 6 minutes or until vegetables are crisp-tender and noodles are tender.

Stir in chicken and pea pods. Simmer, uncovered, for 1 to 2 minutes more or until pea pods are crisp-tender.

Nutrition facts per serving: 224 cal., 6 g total fat (2 g sat. fat), 58 mg chol., 1,280 mg sodium, 17 g carbo., 2 g fiber, 24 g pro. Daily values: 76% vit. A, 82% vit. C, 4% calcium, 19% iron

- 2 14½-ounce cans chicken broth
- 1 cup water
- ¾ cup dried fine egg noodles
- 1 tablespoon soy sauce
- 1 teaspoon grated gingerroot
- ⅛ teaspoon crushed red pepper
- 1 medium red sweet pepper, cut into ¾-inch pieces
- 1 medium carrot, chopped
- ⅓ cup thinly sliced green onions
- 1 cup chopped cooked chicken or turkey
- 1 cup fresh pea pods, halved crosswise, or ½ of a 6-ounce package frozen pea pods, thawed and halved crosswise

fish provençale

The sweet essence of fresh fennel blends nicely with fish, tomatoes, garlic, and onion. This orange-scented soup tastes as good as it smells.

46

8 ounces fresh or frozen skinless haddock, grouper, or halibut fillets

1 small fennel bulb

3 cups vegetable broth or chicken broth

1 large onion, finely chopped

1 small yellow summer squash, cubed (about 1 cup)

1 cup dry white wine

1 teaspoon finely shredded orange or lemon peel

3 cloves garlic, minced

2 cups chopped tomatoes or one 14½-ounce can diced tomatoes

2 tablespoons snipped fresh thyme

Start to finish: 30 minutes   Makes 4 servings (8 cups)

Thaw fish, if frozen. Cut fish into 1-inch pieces; set aside.

Cut off and discard upper stalks of fennel. Remove any wilted outer layers; cut a thin slice from base. Wash fennel; cut in half lengthwise and thinly slice.

In a large saucepan combine fennel, vegetable broth, onion, squash, wine, orange peel, and garlic. Bring to boiling; reduce heat. Simmer, covered, for 10 minutes. Stir in fish pieces, tomatoes, and thyme. Cook about 3 minutes more or just until fish flakes easily. If desired, garnish with additional snipped thyme.

Nutrition facts per serving: 156 cal., 3 g total fat (0 g sat. fat), 18 mg chol., 752 mg sodium, 15 g carbo., 8 g fiber, 14 g pro. Daily values: 11% vit. A, 46% vit. C, 6% calcium, 16% iron

soup with **spirit**

Adding wine to soup often enhances its flavor. Sherry or Madeira blends well with veal or chicken soup. A strongly flavored soup with beef benefits from a tablespoon of dry red table wine. And dry white table wine adds zest to fish soup, crab or lobster bisque, or creamy chowder. Be thrifty with salt in a soup to which wine is added, as the wine intensifies saltiness.

paella soup

Brighten the menu when you serve this colorful soup. From the root of a tropical plant, turmeric gives this rice, shrimp, and pork mixture an inviting yellow glow. Once applied as a perfume many years ago, turmeric is now used to flavor foods.

Start to finish: 35 minutes   Makes 4 servings (6½ cups)

In a large saucepan cook green onions, sweet pepper, and garlic in hot oil 2 minutes.

Stir in chicken broth, rice, bay leaf, salt, red pepper, and turmeric. Heat to boiling; reduce heat. Simmer, covered, for 15 minutes. Stir in the cooked pork, shrimp, and peas. Simmer, covered, for 3 to 5 minutes more or until shrimp turn pink. Remove bay leaf. Stir in fresh oregano.

Nutrition facts per serving: 324 cal., 10 g total fat (3 g sat. fat), 139 mg chol., 879 mg sodium, 25 g carbo., 2 g fiber, 31 g pro. Daily values: 13% vit. A, 29% vit. C, 3% calcium, 25% iron

- ½ cup thinly sliced green onions
- ⅓ cup chopped red sweet pepper
- 1 clove garlic, minced
- 1 teaspoon cooking oil
- 1 14½-ounce can reduced-sodium chicken broth
- ½ cup uncooked long grain rice
- 1 bay leaf
- ¼ teaspoon salt
- ⅛ teaspoon ground red pepper
- ⅛ teaspoon ground turmeric
- 8 ounces cooked pork, cut into ¾-inch cubes
- 8 ounces peeled and deveined fresh shrimp
- 1 cup frozen peas
- 2 teaspoons snipped fresh oregano

sherried smoked salmon soup

Lox-style salmon is the star ingredient in this cream soup. Stir in the flaked, paper-thin strips of brine-cured pink salmon and a touch of sherry and dill just before serving.

- 3 cups sliced fresh shiitake or other mushrooms
- ¾ cup thinly sliced leeks or ½ cup thinly sliced green onions
- 1 tablespoon margarine or butter
- 2 cups chicken broth or vegetable broth
- 2 cups milk
- 2 tablespoons cornstarch
- 4 ounces thinly sliced smoked salmon (lox-style), flaked
- 2 tablespoons dry sherry
- 1 tablespoon snipped fresh dill

Start to finish: 30 minutes   Makes 4 servings (5 cups)

In a large saucepan cook mushrooms and leeks in hot margarine until tender. Stir in chicken broth. Bring to boiling.

Meanwhile, combine milk and cornstarch; stir into mushroom mixture. Cook and stir over medium heat until thickened and bubbly. Cook and stir for 2 minutes more. Stir in salmon, sherry, and dill; heat through.

Nutrition facts per serving: 262 cal., 8 g total fat (3 g sat. fat), 16 mg chol., 722 mg sodium, 35 g carbo., 4 g fiber, 14 g pro. Daily values: 12% vit. A, 14% vit. C, 16% calcium, 15% iron

smoked salmon

Smoked salmon is fresh salmon that has been smoked by either hot- or cold-smoking methods. Lox is brine-cured cold-smoked, which often makes the salmon taste a bit saltier than other smoking methods. Some lox may have a little sugar added to the brine, making it less salty. Look for lox in the seafood section of the supermarket or specialty food shops. Because it is smoked, it is ready to eat.

spicy caramelized
onion soup

A spoonful of sugar really does make these onions cook down in the most delightful way. In addition, the melted sugar adds a rich caramel flavor to the white wine and chicken broth in this flavorful soup.

Start to finish: 30 minutes   Makes 4 servings (5 cups)

In a medium saucepan cook onions and Cajun seasoning in hot oil until onions are tender, stirring frequently. Sprinkle with brown sugar; cook for 1 to 2 minutes more or until onions are golden. Stir in flour; cook for 1 minute more.

Stir in chicken broth, chicken, wine, and pepper; cook and stir until heated through. Top each serving with blue cheese and parsley.

Nutrition facts per serving: 302 cal., 18 g total fat (5 g sat. fat), 48 mg chol., 1,334 mg sodium, 14 g carbo., 1 g fiber, 18 g pro. Daily values: 6% vit. A, 7% vit. C, 6% calcium, 12% iron

3 medium onions, thinly sliced
(about 2¼ cups)

2 teaspoons Cajun seasoning

2 tablespoons cooking oil

1 tablespoon brown sugar

1 tablespoon all-purpose flour

4 cups chicken broth

1½ cups chopped cooked smoked
chicken

¼ cup dry white wine

⅛ teaspoon pepper

¼ cup crumbled blue cheese
or shredded Gruyère cheese
(1 ounce)

1 tablespoon snipped fresh parsley

chicken & shrimp
tortilla soup

Your family will be intrigued when you sprinkle shreds of crisp-baked corn tortillas over the top of this eye-catching Southwestern soup. Make the tortilla shreds ahead of time and store them in an airtight container.

52

6 ounces peeled and deveined fresh or frozen medium shrimp

1 recipe Crisp Tortilla Shreds

1 large onion, chopped

1 teaspoon cumin seed

1 tablespoon cooking oil

4½ cups reduced-sodium chicken broth

1 14½-ounce can Mexican-style stewed tomatoes

3 tablespoons snipped fresh cilantro

2 tablespoons lime juice

1⅔ cups shredded cooked chicken breast

Start to finish: 30 minutes   Makes 6 servings (7¾ cups)

Thaw shrimp, if frozen. Prepare Crisp Tortilla Shreds; set aside.

In a large saucepan cook the onion and cumin seed in hot oil about 5 minutes or until onion is tender. Carefully add chicken broth, undrained tomatoes, cilantro, and lime juice.

Bring to boiling; reduce heat. Simmer, covered, for 8 minutes. Stir in shrimp and chicken. Cook about 3 minutes more or until shrimp turn pink, stirring occasionally. Top each serving with tortilla shreds.

Crisp Tortilla Shreds: Brush four 5½-inch corn tortillas with 1 tablespoon cooking oil. In a small bowl combine ½ teaspoon salt and ⅛ teaspoon pepper; sprinkle mixture over tortillas. Cut tortillas into thin shreds. Arrange in a single layer on a baking sheet. Bake in a 350° oven about 8 minutes or until crisp.

Nutrition facts per serving: 160 cal., 5 g total fat (1 g sat. fat), 80 mg chol., 794 mg sodium, 8 g carbo., 0 g fiber, 21 g pro. Daily values: 7% vit. A, 22% vit. C, 2% calcium, 10% iron

hot & sour turkey soup

The Chinese and Mediterranean technique of cooking egg drops in soup is featured here. The egg cooks in thin, swirling threads as it is stirred slowly into the hot soup.

3½ cups chicken broth

2 cups sliced fresh mushrooms

3 tablespoons rice vinegar
or white vinegar

2 tablespoons soy sauce or
reduced-sodium soy sauce

1 teaspoon sugar

1 teaspoon grated gingerroot

¼ to ½ teaspoon pepper

1 tablespoon cornstarch

1 tablespoon cold water

2 cups shredded cooked turkey

2 cups sliced bok choy

1 6-ounce package frozen pea pods

1 beaten egg

3 tablespoons thinly sliced
green onions

Start to finish: 30 minutes   Makes 4 servings (6⅔ cups)

In a large saucepan combine chicken broth, mushrooms, vinegar, soy sauce, sugar, gingerroot, and pepper. Bring to boiling.

Meanwhile, stir together cornstarch and cold water; stir into broth mixture. Cook and stir until thickened and bubbly. Cook and stir for 2 minutes more. Stir in turkey, bok choy, and pea pods.

Pour the egg into the soup in a steady stream while stirring 2 or 3 times to create shreds. Remove from heat. Stir in green onions.

Nutrition facts per serving: 238 cal., 6 g total fat (2 g sat. fat), 108 mg chol., 1,275 mg sodium, 15 g carbo., 4 g fiber, 30 g pro. Daily values: 4% vit. A, 49% vit. C, 7% calcium, 27% iron

the facts on rice vinegar
Rice vinegar, made from rice wine or sake, has a subtle tang and slightly sweet taste. Chinese rice vinegars are stronger than Japanese vinegars, although both are slightly milder than most vinegars. Chinese rice vinegar comes in three types: white (clear or pale yellow), used mainly in hot-and-sour or sweet-and-sour dishes; red, a typical accompaniment for boiled or steamed shellfish; and black, used mainly as a condiment.

mushroom-noodle
& tofu soup

Japanese udon (oo-DOHN) noodles are similar to spaghetti. Look for them in Asian markets or in the Oriental section of your supermarket.

Start to finish: 30 minutes   Makes 6 servings (9 cups)

In a large saucepan bring the broth to boiling. Meanwhile, in a medium mixing bowl gently stir together tofu cubes, soy sauce, and sesame oil; set aside.

In a medium saucepan cook the sliced mushrooms, gingerroot, and garlic in hot cooking oil for 4 minutes. Add to the hot broth. Stir in the frozen vegetables and udon noodles. Bring to boiling; reduce heat.

Simmer, covered, for 10 to 12 minutes or until vegetables and noodles are tender, stirring once or twice. Gently stir in the tofu mixture and the cilantro; heat through.

Nutrition facts per serving: 162 cal., 7 g total fat (1 g sat. fat), 0 mg chol., 868 mg sodium, 17 g carbo., 1 g fiber, 9 g pro. Daily values: 46% vit. A, 35% vit. C, 3% calcium, 9% iron

- 1 **49-ounce can reduced-sodium chicken broth (about 6 cups)**
- 1 **10- to 12-ounce package extra-firm tofu (fresh bean curd), drained and cut into ½-inch cubes**
- 1 **tablespoon soy sauce**
- 1 **tablespoon toasted sesame oil**
- 6 **ounces sliced fresh shiitake or button mushrooms (about 2¼ cups)**
- 1 **tablespoon grated gingerroot**
- 1 **clove garlic, minced**
- 1 **tablespoon cooking oil**
- 1 **16-ounce package frozen sugar snap stir-fry vegetables**
- 2 **ounces dried udon noodles or spaghetti, broken**
- 1 **tablespoon snipped fresh cilantro**

brandied mushroom soup with herbs

Mushroom lovers will ask for this brandy-and-thyme-seasoned soup time and again. It's a satisfying meal when served over slices of toasted French bread. Just add a tossed green salad and a robust red wine.

3 **cups sliced fresh mushrooms**

1 **medium onion, finely chopped**

1 **tablespoon olive oil**

¼ **cup all-purpose flour**

2 **14½-ounce cans beef broth**

2 **tablespoons brandy or dry white wine (optional)**

1½ **teaspoons snipped fresh thyme or ½ teaspoon dried thyme, crushed**

1 **teaspoon Worcestershire sauce**

2 **tablespoons snipped fresh parsley**

4 **slices toasted French bread (optional)**

Start to finish: 30 minutes   Makes 3 servings (4½ cups)

In a large saucepan cook the mushrooms and onion in hot oil until onion is tender. Stir in flour; gradually stir in beef broth, brandy (if desired), dried thyme (if using), and Worcestershire sauce.

Cook and stir until slightly thickened and bubbly. Cook and stir for 1 minute more. Stir in the parsley and, if using, fresh thyme. If desired, serve over slices of French bread.

Nutrition facts per serving: 125 cal., 6 g total fat (1 g sat. fat), 0 mg chol., 913 mg sodium, 14 g carbo., 2 g fiber, 6 g pro. Daily values: 1% vit. A, 16% vit. C, 3% calcium, 17% iron

marvelous **mushrooms**

There are so many types of mushrooms available at your supermarket. Try experimenting with different varieties. It is usually easy to find the common white or brown mushroom, often referred to as button mushrooms. They are usually very mild in flavor. For a richer, earthier flavor try morels, shiitakes, or portobellos. The best way to clean mushrooms is to brush them off with a clean, soft vegetable brush and wipe them with a clean, damp cloth. Do not soak mushrooms because they're like a sponge and the water will ruin their firm texture.

middle eastern
sausage & beans

Fragrant spices, such as cinnamon and allspice, often flavor Middle Eastern dishes. In this dish, raisins enhance the spices and sausage, adding a delicate, sweet taste. If you like, hot pepper sauce adds heat.

Start to finish: 35 minutes   Makes 4 servings (5½ cups)

In a Dutch oven cook sausage and onion until sausage is no longer pink. Drain well. Stir in cinnamon and allspice; cook for 1 minute.

Stir in the water, kidney beans, and raisins. Bring to boiling; reduce heat. Simmer, covered, for 15 minutes.

Stir in the tomatoes; heat through. If desired, serve with hot pepper sauce.

Nutrition facts per serving: 365 cal., 17 g total fat (6 g sat. fat), 49 mg chol., 764 mg sodium, 38 g carbo., 8 g fiber, 22 g pro. Daily values: 6% vit. A, 41% vit. C, 6% calcium, 21% iron

Note: This also is delicious served over hot cooked rice tossed with toasted pecans.

- 12 ounces bulk hot or mild Italian sausage
- 1½ cups chopped onion
- 1 teaspoon ground cinnamon
- ¼ teaspoon ground allspice
- 2 cups water
- 1 15-ounce can dark red kidney beans, rinsed and drained
- ⅓ cup raisins
- 2 cups chopped tomatoes
- Bottled hot pepper sauce (optional)

garden
varieties

fennel-asparagus soup

Savor the splendor of spring in this garden-fresh soup. Small onions, baby carrots, and tender asparagus partner with baby lima beans for a bowlful of bounty.

Start to finish: 40 minutes   Makes 4 servings (8 cups)

In a Dutch oven combine the chicken broth, lima beans, onions, fennel seed, and pepper. Bring to boiling; reduce heat. Simmer, covered, for 10 minutes. Stir in the carrots and cook for 5 minutes.

Meanwhile, cut off and discard upper stalks of fennel, reserving leaves. Snip ¼ cup fennel leaves; set aside. Remove any wilted outer layers from bulb; cut a thin slice from base. Wash and chop fennel.

Stir the chopped fennel, asparagus, and pancetta into Dutch oven. Cook about 5 minutes more or until vegetables are tender. Garnish each serving with the reserved fennel leaves.

Nutrition facts per serving: 269 cal., 7 g total fat (2 g sat. fat), 8 mg chol., 1,329 mg sodium, 34 g carbo., 15 g fiber, 20 g pro. Daily values: 85% vit. A, 38% vit. C, 7% calcium, 26% iron

6 cups chicken broth

1 10-ounce package frozen baby lima beans

1 cup small red boiling onions, whole pearl onions, or coarsely chopped onion

1 teaspoon fennel seed, crushed

¼ teaspoon pepper

1 cup packaged, peeled baby carrots

1 medium fennel bulb

12 ounces asparagus spears, trimmed and cut into 1-inch pieces

4 ounces pancetta, chopped, crisp-cooked, and drained, or 5 slices bacon, crisp-cooked, drained, and crumbled

turkey & mushroom soup

Orzo pasta thickens this soup of fresh mushrooms and turkey. In Italian, the word "orzo" means barley, but it's actually a tiny pasta shaped like grains of rice.

60

2 cups sliced fresh mushrooms (such as crimini, shiitake, porcini, or button)

1 stalk celery, thinly sliced

1 medium carrot, thinly sliced

1 small onion, chopped

1 tablespoon margarine or butter

4½ cups water

1 tablespoon instant beef bouillon granules

⅛ teaspoon pepper

½ cup dried orzo pasta (rosamarina)

1½ cups chopped cooked turkey

2 tablespoons snipped fresh parsley

1 teaspoon snipped fresh thyme

Start to finish: 35 minutes   Makes 4 servings (6 cups)

In a large saucepan cook mushrooms, celery, carrot, and onion in hot margarine until crisp-tender. Add water, bouillon granules, and pepper.

Bring to boiling; stir in orzo. Return to boiling; reduce heat. Simmer, uncovered, for 5 to 8 minutes or until orzo is tender but still firm. Stir in turkey, parsley, and thyme; heat through.

Nutrition facts per serving: 199 cal., 6 g total fat (2 g sat. fat), 40 mg chol., 767 mg sodium, 17 g carbo, 2 g fiber, 19 g pro. Daily values: 63% vit. A, 10% vit. C, 4% calcium, 17% iron

caraway cabbage-
sausage soup

Here, the nutty, delicate anise flavor of caraway seed is matched with cabbage, apples, and turkey kielbasa. This hearty soup is just what you'll want on a cold winter night.

Start to finish: 30 minutes   Makes 4 servings (7 cups)

In a large saucepan cook cabbage mix, onion, celery, and caraway seed in hot margarine or butter until vegetables are crisp-tender.

Stir in chicken broth, turkey kielbasa, apples, and pepper. Bring to boiling; reduce heat. Simmer, covered, for 5 minutes.

Nutrition facts per serving: 292 cal., 14 g total fat (3 g sat. fat), 57 mg chol., 1,486 mg sodium, 29 g carbo., 6 g fiber, 19 g pro. Daily values: 47% vit. A, 52% vit. C, 6% calcium, 15% iron

- 3 **cups packaged shredded cabbage with carrot (coleslaw mix)**
- 1 **medium onion, chopped**
- 1 **stalk celery, chopped**
- 1½ **teaspoons caraway seed**
- 2 **tablespoons margarine or butter**
- 4 **cups reduced-sodium chicken broth**
- 12 **ounces cooked turkey kielbasa, halved lengthwise and sliced**
- 2 **medium apples, cored and chopped**
- ¼ **teaspoon pepper**

chicken stew with tortellini

Dress up leftover chicken by stirring it into this easy-to-prepare stew. Chunks of yellow squash and sweet pepper accompany plump tortellini and beet greens.

2 cups water

1 14½-ounce can reduced-sodium chicken broth

1 medium yellow summer squash

6 cups torn beet greens, turnip greens, or spinach

1 green sweet pepper, coarsely chopped

1 cup dried cheese-filled tortellini pasta

1 medium onion, cut into thin wedges

1 medium carrot, sliced

1½ teaspoons snipped fresh rosemary

½ teaspoon salt-free seasoning blend

¼ teaspoon pepper

2 cups chopped cooked chicken

1 tablespoon snipped fresh basil

Start to finish: 35 minutes   Makes 6 servings (7½ cups)

In a Dutch oven bring water and chicken broth to boiling. Meanwhile, halve summer squash lengthwise and cut into ½-inch slices. Add squash, greens, sweet pepper, pasta, onion, carrot, rosemary, seasoning blend, and pepper to Dutch oven.

Return to boiling; reduce heat. Simmer, covered, about 15 minutes or until pasta and vegetables are nearly tender.

Stir in chicken. Cook, covered, about 5 minutes more or until pasta and vegetables are tender. Stir fresh basil into soup.

Nutrition facts per serving: 234 cal., 6 g total fat (1 g sat. fat), 45 mg chol., 530 mg sodium, 22 g carbo., 3 g fiber, 22 g pro. Daily values: 114% vit. A, 55% vit. C, 14% calcium, 13% iron

italian greens
& cheese tortellini

Tender spinach and sugar snap peas team with cheese tortellini in this lemon-scented soup. Sprinkle each serving with fresh Parmesan cheese for a sharp flavor accent.

64

1½ cups finely chopped onion

5 cloves garlic, minced

1 teaspoon dried Italian seasoning, crushed

1 tablespoon olive oil

2 14½-ounce cans reduced-sodium chicken broth

1½ cups water

1 9-ounce package refrigerated cheese tortellini

2 cups sugar snap peas, tips and strings removed, halved crosswise

2 cups shredded spinach

2 teaspoons lemon juice

2 tablespoons finely shredded Parmesan cheese

Start to finish: 35 minutes Makes 4 servings (7½ cups)

In a Dutch oven cook onion, garlic, and Italian seasoning in hot oil over medium heat until onion is tender. Add chicken broth and water. Bring to boiling; add tortellini. Return to boiling; reduce heat. Simmer, uncovered, for 4 minutes.

Stir in snap peas, spinach, and lemon juice. Return to boiling; reduce heat. Simmer, uncovered, for 2 minutes more. Top each serving with Parmesan cheese.

Nutrition facts per serving: 320 cal., 10 g total fat (2 g sat. fat), 33 mg chol., 881 mg sodium, 42 g carbo., 4 g fiber, 17 g pro. Daily values: 21% vit. A, 74% vit. C, 18% calcium, 25% iron

roasted red pepper soup

Looking for cooking shortcuts? Grab a jar of roasted red sweet peppers and you'll have the beginning of a bright bowl of soup. Serve this rich cream soup with sesame crackers and a cucumber and tomato salad dressed with a light vinaigrette.

Start to finish: 35 minutes   Makes 5 servings (5½ cups)

In a large saucepan combine chicken broth, roasted peppers, onion, carrot, celery, sugar, and salt. Bring to boiling; reduce heat. Simmer, uncovered, about 15 minutes or until carrot and celery are very tender. Cool slightly.

Place the pepper mixture, half at a time, in a blender container or food processor bowl. Cover and blend or process until smooth. Return the mixture to saucepan. Stir in half-and-half; cook over medium heat until heated through.

Nutrition facts per serving: 229 cal., 13 g total fat (5 g sat. fat), 23 mg chol., 619 mg sodium, 12 g carbo., 3 g fiber, 6 g pro. Daily values: 68% vit. A, 276% vit. C, 7% calcium, 8% iron

- 3 cups chicken broth
- 2 7-ounce jars roasted red sweet peppers, drained and rinsed
- 1 large onion, chopped
- 1 medium carrot, thinly sliced
- 1 stalk celery, thinly sliced
- ¼ teaspoon sugar
- ¼ teaspoon salt
- 1¼ cups half-and-half, light cream, or milk

white bean & pasta soup

Perfect for a Sunday night supper on a cool evening, this meatless soup will satisfy even the most demanding appetites. If you have a meat-loving crew, add 1 to 1½ cups chopped cooked chicken along with the beans.

2 **cups vegetable broth
or chicken broth**

2 **medium carrots, chopped**

1 **medium onion, chopped**

1 **stalk celery, sliced**

⅛ **teaspoon ground white pepper
(optional)**

1 **cup dried radiatore or
mostaccioli**

2 **cups milk**

3 **tablespoons all-purpose flour**

1 **15-ounce can great northern or
white kidney (cannellini)
beans, drained and rinsed**

1 **tablespoon snipped fresh thyme**

1 **cup chopped tomato**

Start to finish: 35 minutes   Makes 4 or 5 servings (6⅔ cups)

In a large saucepan combine the vegetable broth, carrots, onion, celery, and, if desired, white pepper. Bring to boiling; stir in pasta. Return to boiling; reduce heat. Simmer, covered, for 10 to 12 minutes or until pasta is tender but still firm.

Meanwhile, gradually stir milk into flour until smooth; stir flour mixture into pasta mixture. Cook and stir over medium heat until thickened and bubbly. Cook and stir for 2 minutes more. Stir in beans and thyme; heat through. Top individual servings with tomato.

Nutrition facts per serving: 340 cal., 4 g total fat (2 g sat. fat), 10 mg chol., 970 mg sodium, 56 g carbo., 7 g fiber, 19 g pro. Daily values: 127% vit. A, 19% vit. C, 20% calcium, 27% iron

garbanzo bean stew

No need to wait for cooler weather to serve this colorful stew. It is a satisfying meal any time of year. The feta cheese—an optional addition—lends a tangy, fresh flavor.

Start to finish: 20 minutes   Makes 4 servings (6 cups)

In a large covered saucepan cook onion, sweet pepper, and garlic in hot oil until onion is tender, stirring occasionally. Stir in cumin, paprika, and ground red pepper; cook for 1 minute.

Carefully add the water, broth, frozen corn, and oregano. Bring to boiling; reduce heat. Simmer, covered, for 5 to 10 minutes or until corn is tender. Stir in beans, tomato, and lemon juice. Heat through. Ladle into serving bowls. Sprinkle each serving with feta cheese (if desired) and green onion. Makes 4 servings.

Nutrition facts per serving: 217 cal., 6 g total fat (1 g sat. fat), 0 mg chol., 672 mg sodium, 38 g carbo., 5 g fiber, 9 g pro. Daily values: 21% vit. A, 89% vit. C, 6% calcium, 28% iron

- 1 large onion, chopped
- 1 medium green sweet pepper, chopped
- 3 cloves garlic, minced
- 2 teaspoons cooking oil
- 1½ teaspoons ground cumin
- ½ teaspoon paprika
- ⅛ to ¼ teaspoon ground red pepper
- 1½ cups water
- 2 cups reduced-sodium chicken broth
- 1 10-ounce package (2 cups) frozen whole kernel corn
- 2 tablespoons snipped fresh oregano
- 1 15-ounce can garbanzo beans, drained and rinsed
- 1 medium tomato, chopped
- 2 tablespoons lemon juice
- ¼ cup crumbled feta cheese (optional)
- 2 tablespoons thinly sliced green onion

tofu-papaya soup

Papaya and coconut milk lend a mellow sweetness to this refreshing soup, while the gingerroot and cilantro add a spirited flavor. Round out this distinctive soup with a sliced tomato and fresh mozzarella cheese salad and crusty hard rolls.

1 tablespoon grated gingerroot

1 clove garlic, minced

1 tablespoon olive oil

3 cups vegetable broth

1 large papaya, peeled, seeded, and chopped (about 2 cups)

¼ teaspoon bottled hot pepper sauce

½ of a 12-ounce package soft tofu (fresh bean curd), drained and cut into small cubes

2 teaspoons snipped fresh cilantro

¼ cup unsweetened coconut milk

¼ cup chopped peanuts

2 tablespoons chopped green onion

Start to finish: 35 minutes   Makes 3 servings (5 cups)

In a large saucepan cook gingerroot and garlic in hot oil for 2 minutes. Stir in vegetable broth, papaya, and hot pepper sauce. Bring to boiling; reduce heat. Simmer, covered, for 15 minutes.

Stir in the tofu and cilantro. Simmer, covered, for 5 minutes more. Stir in the coconut milk; heat through. Top each serving with peanuts and green onion.

Nutrition facts per serving: 188 cal., 14 g total fat (2 g sat. fat), 0 mg chol., 1,039 mg sodium, 18 g carbo., 2 g fiber, 6 g pro. Daily values: 21% vit. A, 97% vit. C, 3% calcium, 8% iron

the **papaya** puzzle

Ripe papayas are best eaten raw as a fruit, but slightly green papayas can be cooked as a vegetable and are ideal for stirring into soups. Although the pear-shaped papaya can range in size from 1 to 20 pounds, those found most often in the U.S. usually weigh about 1 pound. When ripe, they have a vivid golden-yellow skin. The flesh is a similar color and is juicy and smooth, with a sweet-tart flavor. The large center cavity is full of tiny black seeds; they are edible but usually are discarded.

italian fish &
vegetable soup

When you're in the mood for fish, serve rosemary-scented fish soup. Use any fresh fish that has a firm texture and mild flavor.

Start to finish: 35 minutes Makes 4 servings (7½ cups)

In a large saucepan combine water, undrained tomatoes, cabbage mix, zucchini, celery, onion, wine, bouillon granules, rosemary, bay leaves, and garlic.

Bring to boiling; reduce heat. Simmer, covered, about 10 minutes or until vegetables are crisp-tender. Stir in tomato paste; add fish pieces.

Return to boiling; reduce heat. Simmer, covered, about 5 minutes more or until fish flakes easily with a fork. Remove bay leaves.

Nutrition facts per serving: 153 cal., 1 g total fat (0 g sat. fat), 49 mg chol., 825 mg sodium, 15 g carbo., 4 g fiber, 19 g pro. Daily values: 52% vit. A, 65% vit. C, 8% calcium, 17% iron

convenience counts

When you're cooking meals for your family at the end of a busy day, count on convenience products from the supermarket. Buy precut vegetables, such as the coleslaw mix used here or already-cut vegetables for dips. Also check out the salad bar, which many large supermarkets now provide. Fresh spinach, sliced sweet peppers, broccoli flowerets, and shredded carrots are just a few items you'll find on the salad bar.

3¼ cups water

1 14½-ounce can diced tomatoes

1½ cups packaged shredded cabbage with carrot (coleslaw mix)

1 small zucchini, chopped (about 1 cup)

1 stalk celery, chopped

1 small onion, chopped

¼ cup dry white wine or water

2 teaspoons instant chicken bouillon granules

2 teaspoons snipped fresh rosemary

2 bay leaves

2 cloves garlic, minced

¼ cup tomato paste

12 ounces fresh sea bass, orange roughy, haddock, or cod fillets, cut into 1-inch pieces

tomato-basil soup

This soup is inspired by the cuisine of Northern Italy, where tomatoes and basil are popular ingredients. Try it during the summer months when you can use vegetables and herbs fresh from the garden or farmer's market.

2   medium carrots, finely chopped

2   stalks celery, finely chopped

1   large onion, finely chopped

6   cloves garlic, minced

1   tablespoon olive oil

1   cup water

2   pounds tomatoes, chopped
    (about 6 cups)

½   cup snipped fresh basil or
    2 tablespoons dried basil,
    crushed, plus ½ cup snipped
    fresh parsley

1   teaspoon salt

1   tablespoon balsamic vinegar

Start to finish: 40 minutes   Makes 4 servings (6 cups)

In a large saucepan cook carrots, celery, onion, and garlic, covered, in hot oil over medium-low heat for 10 minutes, stirring occasionally. Transfer to a blender container or food processor bowl; add the water. Cover and blend or process until smooth. Return to pan.

Stir in half of the tomatoes, half of the fresh basil or all of the dried basil, and the salt. Bring to boiling; reduce heat. Simmer, covered, for 15 minutes. Remove from heat.

Stir in the remaining tomatoes, the remaining fresh basil or all of the parsley, and the balsamic vinegar; heat through.

Nutrition facts per serving: 145 cal., 5 g total fat (1 g sat. fat), 0 mg chol., 618 mg sodium, 26 g carbo., 6 g fiber, 4 g pro. Daily values: 101% vit. A, 116% vit. C, 5% calcium, 14% iron

choice chowders

spicy pumpkin & shrimp soup

During the week, convenience is key. Here's a way to turn a can of pumpkin into an exciting soup. Just the right blend of ginger, cilantro, allspice, and garlic complement the pumpkin for a terrific flavor.

Start to finish: 30 minutes   Makes 4 servings (5¾ cups)

In a large saucepan cook onions, carrots, cilantro, gingerroot, garlic, and allspice, covered, in hot margarine or butter for 10 to 12 minutes or until vegetables are tender, stirring once or twice.

Transfer the mixture to a blender container or food processor bowl. Add ½ cup of the chicken broth. Cover and blend or process until nearly smooth.

In same saucepan combine pumpkin, milk, and remaining broth. Stir in blended vegetable mixture and shrimp; heat through. If desired, thread additional cooked shrimp on small skewers; top each serving with a spoonful of yogurt, snipped chives, and the skewered cooked shrimp.

Nutrition facts per serving: 222 cal., 9 g total fat (2 g sat. fat), 116 mg chol., 579 mg sodium, 19 g carbo., 5 g fiber, 18 g pro. Daily values: 329% vit. A, 15% vit. C, 12% calcium, 25% iron

on the thaw
It is unsafe to thaw fish, seafood, or any type of meat at room temperature. Thaw them in one of two ways: 1. The best way to thaw is to place the unopened original container in the refrigerator overnight. 2. Place the wrapped package under *cold* running water until thawed.

- 2 **medium onions, sliced**
- 2 **medium carrots, thinly sliced**
- 1 **tablespoon snipped fresh cilantro**
- 2 **teaspoons grated gingerroot**
- 2 **cloves garlic, minced**
- ½ **teaspoon ground allspice**
- 2 **tablespoons margarine or butter**
- 1 **14½-ounce can chicken broth**
- 1 **15-ounce can pumpkin**
- 1 **cup milk**
- 1 **8-ounce package frozen, peeled and deveined cooked shrimp, thawed**
-    **Additional shrimp in shells, peeled, deveined, and cooked (optional)**
-    **Plain low-fat yogurt or dairy sour cream (optional)**
-    **Snipped fresh chives (optional)**

caribbean clam chowder

Clams combine with sweet potatoes, tomatoes, chile peppers, and a hint of lime and rum to make a soup full of exuberant flavor.

74

½ pint shucked clams
    or one 6½-ounce can
    minced clams

2 cups peeled and cubed sweet
    potatoes (1 to 2 medium)

1 medium onion, chopped

1 stalk celery, chopped

¼ cup chopped red sweet pepper

2 cloves garlic, minced

1½ teaspoons snipped fresh
    thyme or ½ teaspoon
    dried thyme, crushed

1 10-ounce can chopped tomatoes
    and green chile peppers

1 tablespoon lime juice

1 tablespoon dark rum (optional)

Start to finish: 35 minutes   Makes 4 servings (6 cups)

Drain clams, reserving juice. Add enough water to clam juice to make 2½ cups liquid. If using fresh clams, chop clams; set aside.

In a large saucepan bring the clam liquid to boiling. Stir in the sweet potatoes, onion, celery, sweet pepper, garlic, and, if using, dried thyme. Return to boiling; reduce heat. Simmer, covered, about 10 minutes or until sweet potatoes are tender.

Mash mixture slightly with a potato masher. Stir in clams, undrained tomatoes, lime juice, rum (if desired), and, if using, fresh thyme. Return to boiling; reduce heat. Cook for 1 to 2 minutes more.

Nutrition facts per serving: 128 cal., 1 g total fat (0 g sat. fat), 19 mg chol., 337 mg sodium, 22 g carbo., 3 g fiber, 9 g pro. Daily values: 141% vit. A, 66% vit. C, 6% calcium, 57% iron

oyster & corn chowder

If you think a fresh oyster chowder will take too long to make, this soup will surprise you. Buy oysters already shucked from the seafood section of the supermarket. They cook in just 5 minutes to create a creamy jalapeño-spiced chowder.

Start to finish: 40 minutes   Makes 3 servings (4 cups)

In a medium saucepan cook onion, sweet pepper, and garlic in hot oil over medium heat until vegetables are tender. Carefully stir in chicken broth, potato or rice, jalapeño peppers, salt, and black pepper. Bring to boiling; reduce heat.

Simmer, covered, about 10 minutes or until potato or rice is nearly tender. Stir in undrained oysters, corn, and oregano. Return to boiling; reduce heat.

Simmer, covered, about 5 minutes or until oysters are plump and opaque. Stir in half-and-half; heat through.

Nutrition facts per serving: 312 cal., 13 g total fat (4 g sat. fat), 57 mg chol., 596 mg sodium, 39 g carbo., 4 g fiber, 13 g pro. Daily values: 26% vit. A, 84% vit. C, 8% calcium, 41% iron

don't let the **heat** get to **you!**
When handling jalapeño peppers or other fresh chile peppers, wear rubber or plastic gloves to prevent skin burns. Disposable plastic gloves are ideal and inexpensive. You can purchase them in pharmacies and paint stores. If skin burns should occur, wash the area well with soapy water. If the juices come in contact with the eyes, flush them with cool water to neutralize the chile pepper oil.

- 1 large onion, chopped
- ½ cup chopped red sweet pepper
- 1 garlic clove, minced
- 1 tablespoon olive oil
- 1 14½-ounce can chicken broth
- 1½ cups chopped potato or ¼ cup uncooked long grain rice
- 1 or 2 fresh jalapeño peppers, seeded and finely chopped
- Dash salt
- Dash black pepper
- 8 ounces shucked oysters with their liquid
- 1 cup fresh or frozen whole kernel corn
- 1 tablespoon snipped fresh oregano
- ½ cup half-and-half or light cream

crab chowder

This winning chowder features the prize of all seafood—crabmeat. It's even more enticing with bouquet garni seasoning—a mixture of several herbs—and a small amount of cream cheese.

1 6-ounce package frozen
   crabmeat or one 6-ounce
   can crabmeat, drained, flaked,
   and cartilage removed

1 medium zucchini, cut into
   2-inch strips

1 medium red or green sweet
   pepper, chopped

2 tablespoons margarine or butter

2 tablespoons all-purpose flour

4 cups milk

2 tablespoons sliced green onion

½ teaspoon bouquet garni seasoning

¼ teaspoon salt

⅛ teaspoon black pepper

1 3-ounce package cream cheese,
   cut up

1 teaspoon snipped fresh thyme

   Fresh thyme sprigs (optional)

Start to finish: 25 minutes   Makes 4 servings (5 cups)

Thaw crabmeat, if frozen.

In a medium saucepan cook zucchini and sweet pepper in hot margarine or butter until crisp-tender. Stir in the flour. Add the milk, green onion, bouquet garni seasoning, salt, and black pepper.

Cook and stir over medium-high heat until thickened and bubbly. Add the cream cheese; cook and stir until cream cheese melts. Stir in the crabmeat and snipped thyme; heat through. If desired, garnish each serving with additional fresh thyme.

Nutrition facts per serving: 314 cal., 19 g total fat (9 g sat. fat), 64 mg chol., 844 mg sodium, 18 g carbo., 1 g fiber, 19 g pro. Daily values: 34% vit. A, 36% vit. C, 29% calcium, 8% iron

southern ham chowder

Southern cooks are renowned for pairing ham with vegetables. In this creamy chowder, smoky bits of cooked ham simmer with yellow squash, red sweet pepper, potato, and green onions.

1½ **cups thinly sliced yellow summer squash or zucchini**

½ **cup chopped red or green sweet pepper**

½ **teaspoon dried thyme, crushed**

1 **tablespoon margarine or butter**

2 **cups water**

1½ **cups chopped potato**

Dash black pepper

6 **ounces thinly sliced cooked ham or turkey ham, chopped**

¾ **cup finely chopped green onions**

½ **cup half-and-half or light cream**

Start to finish: 35 minutes Makes 3 or 4 servings (5 cups)

In a large saucepan cook the squash, sweet pepper, and thyme in hot margarine or butter over medium heat about 3 minutes or until squash is tender. Add water, potato, and pepper.

Bring to boiling; reduce heat. Simmer, covered, for 12 to 15 minutes or until potato is tender. Remove from heat. Mash slightly with a potato masher. Stir in ham, green onions, and half-and-half; heat through.

Nutrition facts per serving: 261 cal., 12 g total fat (5 g sat. fat), 45 mg chol., 755 mg sodium, 23 g carbo., 2 g fiber, 16 g pro. Daily values: 28% vit. A, 95% vit. C, 7% calcium, 18% iron

what's the difference?

Do you know the difference between a chowder and a bisque? A chowder typically is a thick, milk- or cream-based soup that contains a variety of seafood and vegetables. It also describes a thick, rich chunky soup. Chowders often are thickened with potatoes or a roux, a flour and fat mixture. A bisque is a thick, rich, and creamy soup made of puréed shellfish or fish, and, sometimes, meat or vegetables. Traditionally, it is thickened with rice.

vegetable cheese chowder

Frozen vegetables are the secret to this quick chowder. A little smoked Gouda cheese produces the robust flavor.

Start to finish: 20 minutes   Makes 4 servings (6 cups)

In a large saucepan combine the frozen vegetables and water. Bring to boiling; reduce heat. Simmer, covered, about 4 minutes or until vegetables are just tender. Do not drain.

Meanwhile, in a screw-top jar combine ⅔ cup of the milk, the flour, and pepper; cover and shake well. Add to saucepan; add the remaining milk and chicken broth. Cook and stir until thickened and bubbly. Cook and stir for 1 minute more. Add the Gouda cheese; cook and stir over low heat until cheese nearly melts.

Nutrition facts per serving: 370 cal., 20 g total fat (13 g sat. fat), 81 mg chol., 942 mg sodium, 22 g carbo., 3 g fiber, 25 g pro. Daily values: 162% vit. A, 72% vit. C, 52% calcium, 9% iron

- 1 **16-ounce package loose-pack frozen broccoli, cauliflower, and carrots**
- ½ **cup water**
- 2 **cups milk**
- ⅓ **cup all-purpose flour**
- ⅛ **teaspoon pepper**
- 1 **14½-ounce can chicken broth**
- 1 **cup shredded smoked or regular Gouda cheese (4 ounces)**

jalapeño corn chowder

Spectacular and rich, this chowder features the popular Southwestern flavors of corn, jalapeño peppers, and red sweet peppers. Although not a must, crumbled feta cheese sprinkled over each serving adds a salty tang to the soup.

Start to finish: 20 minutes   Makes 4 servings (5 cups)

In a blender container or food processor bowl combine half of the corn and the chicken broth. Cover and blend or process until nearly smooth.

In a large saucepan combine the broth mixture and the remaining corn. If using fresh corn, bring to boiling; reduce heat. Simmer, covered, for 2 to 3 minutes or until corn is crisp-tender.

Stir in cooked pasta, milk, roasted peppers, and jalapeño peppers; heat through. If desired, top each serving with feta cheese.

Nutrition facts per serving: 247 cal., 3 g total fat (1 g sat. fat), 5 mg chol., 363 mg sodium, 47 g carbo., 1 g fiber, 11 g pro. Daily values: 10% vit. A, 61% vit. C, 7% calcium, 13% iron

3 cups frozen whole kernel corn or 3 cups fresh corn kernels (cut from 6 to 7 ears of corn)

1 14½-ounce can chicken broth

1¼ cups cooked small pasta (such as ditalini or tiny shell macaroni)

1 cup milk, half-and-half, or light cream

¼ of a 7-ounce jar roasted red sweet peppers, drained and chopped (¼ cup)

1 or 2 fresh jalapeño peppers, seeded and finely chopped

½ cup crumbled feta cheese (optional)

turkey & wild rice chowder

If you yearn for the nutty flavor of wild rice, but time is short, substitute quick-cooking long grain and wild rice mix, omitting the seasoning packet.

6 ounces cooked smoked turkey sausage links

2 cups milk

1½ cups water

1 medium onion, chopped

½ cup chopped red or green sweet pepper

½ cup frozen whole kernel corn

2 teaspoons instant chicken bouillon granules

2 teaspoons snipped fresh marjoram or ½ teaspoon dried marjoram, crushed

¼ teaspoon black pepper

2 tablespoons all-purpose flour

1½ cups cooked wild or brown rice

Start to finish: 25 minutes   Makes 4 servings (5¾ cups)

Cut turkey sausage links in half lengthwise; cut into ½-inch-thick slices. In a large saucepan combine the sausage, 1¾ cups of the milk, the water, onion, sweet pepper, corn, bouillon granules, dried marjoram (if using), and black pepper. Bring to boiling.

Meanwhile, combine flour and remaining ¼ cup milk. Stir into turkey mixture. Cook and stir until thickened and bubbly. Cook and stir for 1 minute more. Stir in the cooked rice and, if using, fresh marjoram; heat through.

Nutrition facts per serving: 236 cal., 7 g total fat (3 g sat. fat), 40 mg chol., 742 mg sodium, 30 g carbo., 2 g fiber, 15 g pro. Daily values: 8% vit. A, 16% vit. C, 15% calcium, 9% iron

rice for later

When you have the time—and to save time later—cook extra rice and save it. Place cooked rice in an airtight container and store it in the refrigerator for up to 1 week or in the freezer for up to 6 months. Generally, 1 cup of uncooked brown or white rice will yield 3 cups of cooked rice. One cup of wild rice will yield about 2⅔ cups of cooked wild rice.

roasted garlic turkey chowder

Opt for convenience when you select this chowder. Count on the fresh vegetables, turkey, and basil to round out the roasted garlic flavor.

Start to finish: 30 minutes   Makes 4 servings (6 cups)

In a large saucepan combine broccoli, carrot, potato, water, and onion. Bring to boiling; reduce heat. Simmer, covered, about 6 minutes or until vegetables are tender. Do not drain.

Stir in milk, turkey, condensed soup, and basil. Cook and stir over medium heat until heated through.

Nutrition facts per serving: 269 cal., 9 g total fat (3 g sat. fat), 53 mg chol., 419 mg sodium, 24 g carbo., 4 g fiber, 22 g pro. Daily values: 53% vit. A, 56% vit. C, 15% calcium, 8% iron

1 cup small broccoli flowerets

1 medium carrot, shredded

½ cup chopped peeled potato or ½ cup loose-pack frozen diced hash-brown potatoes

½ cup water

¼ cup chopped onion

2 cups milk

1½ cups chopped cooked turkey or chicken

1 10½-ounce can condensed cream of roasted garlic soup

1½ teaspoons snipped fresh basil

souper quick simmers

pesto-vegetable soup

A swirl of basil pesto provides the perfect flavor accent for this vegetable and pasta soup. Pesto can be purchased already prepared at your supermarket or deli.

Start to finish: 25 minutes   Makes 3 servings (5 cups)

In a large saucepan cook garlic in hot oil for 30 seconds. Add vegetable broth. Bring to boiling; add pasta. Return to boiling; reduce heat. Boil gently, uncovered, for 6 minutes, stirring occasionally.

Stir in stir-fry vegetables; return to boiling. Stir in arugula and spinach; cook and stir for 2 minutes more. Swirl pesto into each serving.

Nutrition facts per serving: 261 cal., 17 g total fat (1 g sat. fat), 2 mg chol., 1,281 mg sodium, 29 g carbo., 1 g fiber, 7 g pro. Daily values: 63% vit. A, 40% vit. C, 7% calcium, 15% iron

2 cloves garlic, minced

1 tablespoon olive oil

2 14½-ounce cans vegetable broth

½ cup dried ditalini pasta or small shells pasta

1 cup packaged frozen stir-fry vegetables

3 cups torn arugula, torn Swiss chard, or shredded Chinese cabbage

2 cups torn spinach

3 tablespoons pesto

curried chicken soup

This spiced chicken noodle soup can be ready in just 20 minutes. You can use leftover cooked chicken, or buy a roasted chicken from your supermarket's deli.

5 cups water

1 3-ounce package chicken-flavored
   ramen noodles

2 to 3 teaspoons curry powder

1 cup sliced fresh mushrooms

2 cups cubed cooked chicken

1 medium apple, cored and
   coarsely chopped

½ cup canned sliced water chestnuts

Start to finish: 20 minutes   Makes 5 servings (6½ cups)

In a large saucepan combine water, the flavoring packet from noodles, and curry powder. Bring to boiling.

Break up noodles. Add noodles and mushrooms to mixture in saucepan; reduce heat. Simmer, uncovered, for 3 minutes. Stir in chicken, apple, and water chestnuts; heat through.

Nutrition facts per serving: 221 cal., 8 g total fat (1 g sat. fat), 54 mg chol., 362 mg sodium, 17 g carbo., 1 g fiber, 20 g pro. Daily values: 1% vit. A, 4% vit. C, 2% calcium, 10% iron

chicken & rosemary soup

Comfort food? Yes. Ordinary? No. Fresh rosemary, assorted vegetables, chicken, and shredded Parmesan cheese make this cream soup a favorite.

87

Start to finish: 25 minutes   Makes 4 servings (5 cups)

In a large saucepan cook onion in hot oil until tender. Stir in chicken broth and pepper. Bring to boiling.

Meanwhile, stir together milk and cornstarch until smooth. Add milk mixture to broth mixture. Stir in squash, peas, and rosemary. Cook and stir until thickened and bubbly. Reduce heat; cook and stir for 2 minutes more. Stir in chicken and Parmesan cheese; heat through.

Nutrition facts per serving: 412 cal., 18 g total fat (7 g sat. fat), 82 mg chol., 610 mg sodium, 24 g carbo., 3 g fiber, 37 g pro. Daily values: 19% vit. A, 16% vit. C, 36% calcium, 15% iron

1	large onion, chopped
2	teaspoons olive oil or cooking oil
1	cup chicken broth
⅛	teaspoon pepper
3	cups milk
4	teaspoons cornstarch
1	small yellow summer squash or zucchini, quartered lengthwise and sliced
1	cup frozen peas
1½	teaspoons snipped fresh rosemary
2	cups chopped cooked chicken
½	cup finely shredded Parmesan cheese

turkey tortilla soup

Put a Mexican twist on turkey by combining it with tomatoes, succotash, jalapeño pepper, and cilantro. This bold-flavored soup is thickened with a surprise ingredient—crumbled tortilla chips.

2 teaspoons chili powder

1 teaspoon cooking oil

3 cups chicken broth

1 14½-ounce can Mexican-style stewed tomatoes

1 10-ounce package frozen succotash

2 cups broken tortilla chips

1 fresh jalapeño pepper, seeded and chopped

2 cups chopped cooked turkey or chicken

¼ cup snipped fresh cilantro

Chopped avocado (optional)

Start to finish: 25 minutes   Makes 4 servings (7 cups)

In a large heavy saucepan cook the chili powder in hot oil over low heat for 1 minute, stirring frequently. Carefully stir in chicken broth and undrained tomatoes. Bring to boiling.

Stir in succotash, ⅓ cup of the tortilla chips, and the jalapeño pepper. Return to boiling; reduce heat. Simmer, covered, about 10 minutes or until succotash is tender.

Stir in the turkey and cilantro; heat through. Top each serving with remaining tortilla chips and, if desired, avocado.

Nutrition facts per serving: 462 cal., 18 g total fat (4 g sat. fat), 59 mg chol., 1,192 mg sodium, 45 g carbo., 6 g fiber, 32 g pro. Daily values: 16% vit. A, 47% vit. C, 6% calcium, 23% iron

sesame beef &
sugar snap pea soup

It only takes a little sesame oil to add an Oriental accent to this soup. The nutty flavored oil works its magic on a colorful combination of sugar snap peas, yellow pepper, green onions, and beef.

Start to finish: 20 minutes   Makes 4 servings (6 cups)

In a large saucepan combine beef broth, water, snap peas, sweet pepper, green onions, sesame oil, and gingerroot. Bring to boiling; reduce heat. Simmer, covered, for 4 to 5 minutes or until vegetables are crisp-tender. Stir in cooked beef and vinegar; heat through. Serve over rice.

Nutrition facts per serving: 274 cal., 7 g total fat (2 g sat. fat), 49 mg chol., 712 mg sodium, 27 g carbo., 1 g fiber, 23 g pro. Daily values: 2% vit. A, 105% vit. C, 3% calcium, 25% iron

2 14½-ounce cans beef broth

1 cup water

1 cup sugar snap peas, strings
     and tips removed

⅓ cup chopped yellow sweet pepper

⅓ cup thinly sliced green onions

1½ teaspoons toasted sesame oil

1 teaspoon grated gingerroot

8 ounces cooked beef, cut into
     bite-size pieces (about 1½ cups)

2 tablespoons rice vinegar or
     white vinegar

2 cups hot cooked rice

lemon & scallop soup

Long-stemmed, tiny-capped, and slightly crunchy, enoki mushrooms play an important role in Asian cooking. These elegant mushrooms have a light, fruity flavor. Toss a few into the soup at the last moment, as they will toughen if heated.

12 ounces fresh or frozen bay scallops

5 cups reduced-sodium
    chicken broth

½ cup dry white wine or
    reduced-sodium chicken broth

3 tablespoons snipped fresh cilantro

2 teaspoons finely shredded
    lemon peel

¼ teaspoon pepper

1 pound asparagus spears, trimmed
    and cut into bite-size pieces

1 cup fresh enoki mushrooms
    or shiitake mushrooms

½ cup sliced green onions

1 tablespoon lemon juice

Start to finish: 25 minutes   Makes 4 servings (7 cups)

Thaw scallops, if frozen. Rinse well and drain.

In a large saucepan combine the chicken broth, wine, cilantro, lemon peel, and pepper. Bring to boiling.

Add the drained scallops, asparagus, shiitake mushrooms (if using), and green onions. Return just to boiling; reduce heat.

Simmer, uncovered, about 5 minutes or until asparagus is tender and scallops are opaque. Remove from heat. Stir in the enoki mushrooms (if using) and lemon juice. Serve immediately.

Nutrition facts per serving: 153 cal., 2 g total fat (0 g sat. fat), 28 mg chol., 940 mg sodium, 10 g carbo., 2 g fiber, 20 g pro. Daily values: 9% vit. A, 50% vit. C, 3% calcium, 6% iron

quick cioppino

San Francisco's Italian immigrants are credited with creating the original cioppino (chuh-PEE-noh). This version of the delicious fish stew is very easy to make.

1 medium green sweet pepper, cut into thin bite-size strips

1 large onion, chopped

2 cloves garlic, minced

1 tablespoon olive oil or cooking oil

2 14½-ounce cans Italian-style stewed tomatoes

½ cup water

6 ounces fresh cod fillets, cut into 1-inch pieces

6 ounces peeled and deveined fresh shrimp

3 tablespoons snipped fresh basil

Start to finish: 20 minutes   Makes 4 servings (5½ cups)

In a large saucepan cook sweet pepper, onion, and garlic in hot oil until tender. Stir in undrained tomatoes and water. Bring to boiling.

Stir in cod and shrimp. Return to boiling; reduce heat. Simmer, covered, for 2 to 3 minutes or until the cod flakes easily and shrimp turn pink. Stir in the basil.

Nutrition facts per serving: 176 cal., 4 g total fat (1 g sat. fat), 82 mg chol., 819 mg sodium, 19 g carbo., 1 g fiber, 17 g pro. Daily values: 20% vit. A, 67% vit. C, 5% calcium, 13% iron

is the **catch fresh?**

When buying fresh fish, look for a bright color and a sweet, not fishy smell. If possible, buy a whole fish; then cut it up and store what you don't use. Look for slightly bulging eyes and brightly colored gills. Fish steaks or fillets should be firm and moist. Don't buy fish that is off-color or brown on the edges.

Since most of the shrimp available today has been previously frozen, always check to see if defrosted shrimp is firm and shiny. When purchasing frozen shrimp, make sure it is frozen solidly and has little or no odor, no brown spots, and no signs of freezer burn, indicated by a white, dry appearance around the edges. Frozen shrimp should be thawed overnight in the refrigerator or placed under cold running water. Do not thaw at room temperature.

endive, ham, & bean soup

Curly endive, often mistaken for chicory, grows in loose heads with lacy, green-rimmed outer leaves that curl at the tips. It is used mainly in salads, but here it is cooked briefly and enjoyed in a tasty bean soup.

93

Start to finish: 25 minutes   Makes 4 servings (6 cups)

In a large saucepan cook onion, carrot, celery, and garlic in hot oil until tender. Stir in chicken broth, kidney beans, ham, and sage.

Bring to boiling. Stir in curly endive; reduce heat. Simmer, covered, about 3 minutes or just until endive wilts.

Nutrition facts per serving: 226 cal., 6 g total fat (1 g sat. fat), 13 mg chol., 1,281 mg sodium, 33 g carbo., 11 g fiber, 20 g pro. Daily values: 66% vit. A, 10% vit. C, 7% calcium, 18% iron

1 medium onion, chopped

1 medium carrot, chopped

1 stalk celery, chopped

2 cloves garlic, minced

1 tablespoon olive oil or cooking oil

4 cups reduced-sodium chicken broth

1 19-ounce can white kidney (cannellini) beans, rinsed and drained

⅔ cup chopped cooked ham

¾ teaspoon dried sage, crushed

3 cups shredded curly endive or Chinese cabbage

Allspice Meatball Stew, 7

apples
Caraway Cabbage-Sausage Soup, 61
Moroccan Lamb Tagine, 11
Asian Chicken Noodle Soup, 45

asparagus
Asparagus and Cheese Potato Soup, 21
Fennel-Asparagus Soup, 59
Lemon and Scallop Soup, 90
Bayou Shrimp Soup, 23

beans
Black and White Bean Chili, 22
Chicken Chili with Rice, 37
Easy Cassoulet, 8
Endive, Ham, and Bean Soup, 93
Garbanzo Bean Stew, 67
Garlic, Black Bean, and Sausage Soup, 31
Greek Minestrone, 12
Middle Eastern Sausage and Beans, 57
White Bean and Pasta Soup, 66
Beef and Sugar Snap Pea Soup, Sesame, 89
Black and White Bean Chili, 22
Brandied Mushroom Soup with Herbs, 56

cabbage
Caraway Cabbage-Sausage Soup, 61
Gingered Pork and Cabbage Soup, 29
Cajun Fish Soup, 43
Caraway Cabbage-Sausage Soup, 61
Caribbean Clam Chowder, 74
Caribbean-Style Pork Stew, 32
Cassoulet, Easy, 8

cheese
Asparagus and Cheese Potato Soup, 21
Potato Soup with Blue Cheese, 17
Vegetable Cheese Chowder, 79

chicken
Asian Chicken Noodle Soup, 45
Chicken and Rice Soup with Dumplings, 27
Chicken and Rosemary Soup, 87
Chicken and Shrimp Tortilla Soup, 52
Chicken Chili with Rice, 37
Chicken Stew with Tortellini, 62
Chipotle Chile Pepper Soup, 38
Creamy Chicken Vegetable Soup, 26
Curried Chicken Soup, 86
Easy Cassoulet, 8
Spicy Caramelized Onion Soup, 51
Yucatan Soup with Lime, 34

chili
Black and White Bean Chili, 22
Chicken Chili with Rice, 37
Chinese Glass Noodle Soup, 30
Chipotle Chile Pepper Soup, 38
Chunky Ratatouille Stew, 15
Cioppino, Quick, 92

Clam Chowder, Caribbean, 74

corn
Jalapeño Corn Chowder, 81
Oyster and Corn Chowder, 75
Pork and Hominy Stew, 10
Pork, Corn, and Three-Pepper Soup, 35
Crab Chowder, 76
Creamy Chicken Vegetable Soup, 26
Crisp Tortilla Shreds, 52

curry
Curried Chicken Soup, 86
Curried Lentil Soup, 18
Mushroom Tortelloni in Curry Cream, 40
Thai Red Curry Soup with Shrimp, 42
Dumplings, 27
Easy Cassoulet, 8
Endive, Ham, and Bean Soup, 93
Fennel-Asparagus Soup, 59
Fish Provençal, 46

fish and shellfish. *See also* Shrimp
Cajun Fish Soup, 43
Caribbean Clam Chowder, 74
Crab Chowder, 76
Fish Provençale, 46
Italian Fish and Vegetable Soup, 69
Lemon and Scallop Soup, 90
Oyster and Corn Chowder, 75
Quick Cioppino, 92
Sherried Smoked Salmon Soup, 50
Garbanzo Bean Stew, 67

garlic
Garlic, Black Bean, and Sausage Soup, 31
Roasted Garlic-Turkey Chowder, 83
Gingered Pork and Cabbage Soup, 29
Greek Minestrone, 12

greens
Chicken Stew with Tortellini, 62
Italian Greens and Cheese Tortellini, 64
Shrimp and Greens Soup, 25

ham
Endive, Ham, and Bean Soup, 93
Southern Ham Chowder, 78
Hot and Sour Turkey Soup, 54
Italian Fish and Vegetable Soup, 69
Italian Greens and Cheese Tortellini, 64
Jalapeño Corn Chowder, 81
Lamb Tagine, Moroccan, 11
Lemon and Scallop Soup, 90
Lentil Soup, Curried, 18
Meatball Stew, Allspice, 7
Middle Eastern Sausage and Beans, 57
Minestrone, Greek, 12
Moroccan Lamb Tagine, 11
Mushroom Tortelloni in Curry Cream, 40

mushrooms
Brandied Mushroom Soup with Herbs, 56
Lemon and Scallop Soup, 90
Mushroom-Noodle and Tofu Soup, 55
Mushroom Tortelloni in Curry Cream, 40
Sherried Smoked Salmon Soup, 50
Turkey and Mushroom Soup, 60
Wild Rice, Barley, and Mushroom Soup, 16

noodles
Asian Chicken Noodle Soup, 45
Chinese Glass Noodle Soup, 30
Mushroom Noodle and Tofu Soup, 55
Onion Soup, Spicy Caramelized, 51
Oyster and Corn Chowder, 75
Paella Soup, 49

pasta. *See also* Noodles
Chicken Stew with Tortellini, 62
Italian Greens and Cheese Tortellini, 64
Mushroom Tortelloni in Curry Cream, 40
White Bean and Pasta Soup, 66

peppers, chile
Chipotle Chile Pepper Soup, 38
Jalapeño Corn Chowder, 81
Pork, Corn, and Three-Pepper Soup, 35

peppers, sweet
Pork, Corn, and Three-Pepper Soup, 35
Roasted Red Pepper Soup, 65
Pesto-Vegetable Soup, 85

pork. *See also* Ham, Sausage
Caribbean-Style Pork Stew, 32
Chinese Glass Noodle Soup, 30
Gingered Pork and Cabbage Soup, 29
Paella Soup, 49
Pork and Hominy Stew, 10
Pork, Corn, and Three-Pepper Soup, 35

potatoes
Asparagus and Cheese Potato Soup, 21
Potato Soup with Blue Cheese, 17
Pumpkin and Shrimp Soup, Spicy, 73
Quick Cioppino, 92
Ratatouille Stew, Chunky, 15

rice. *See also* Wild rice
Chicken and Rice Soup with Dumplings, 27
Chicken Chili with Rice, 37
Paella Soup, 49
Roasted Garlic-Turkey Chowder, 83
Roasted Red Pepper Soup, 65

sausage
Bayou Shrimp Soup, 23
Caraway Cabbage-Sausage Soup, 61
Easy Cassoulet, 8
Garlic, Black Bean, and Sausage Soup, 31
Middle Eastern Sausage and Beans, 57
Sausage and Vegetable Soup, 9

Sesame Beef and Sugar Snap Pea Soup, 89
Sherried Smoked Salmon Soup, 50
shrimp
  Bayou Shrimp Soup, 23
  Cajun Fish Soup, 43
  Chicken and Shrimp Tortilla Soup, 52
  Paella Soup, 49
  Quick Cioppino, 92
  Shrimp and Greens Soup, 25
  Spicy Pumpkin and Shrimp Soup, 73
  Thai Red Curry Soup with Shrimp, 42
Smoked Salmon Soup, Sherried, 50
Southern Ham Chowder, 78
Spicy Caramelized Onion Soup, 51
Spicy Pumpkin and Shrimp Soup, 73
Sugar Snap Pea Soup, Sesame Beef and, 89
Thai Red Curry Soup with Shrimp, 42
tofu
  Mushroom-Noodle and Tofu Soup, 55
  Tofu-Papaya Soup, 68
tomatoes
  Bayou Shrimp Soup, 23
  Tomato-Basil Soup, 70
tortillas
  Chicken and Shrimp Tortilla Soup, 52
  Crisp Tortilla Shreds, 52
  Turkey Tortilla Soup, 88
turkey. *See* also Sausage
  Hot and Sour Turkey Soup, 54
  Roasted Garlic-Turkey Chowder, 83
  Turkey and Mushroom Soup, 60
  Turkey and Wild Rice Chowder, 82
  Turkey Tortilla Soup, 88
vegetables. *See* also specific vegetable
  Allspice Meatball Stew, 7
  Caribbean-Style Pork Stew, 32
  Chicken and Rosemary Soup, 87
  Chicken Stew with Tortellini, 62
  Chunky Ratatouille Stew, 15
  Creamy Chicken Vegetable Soup, 26
  Fish Provençale, 46
  Garbanzo Bean Stew, 67
  Greek Minestrone, 12
  Italian Fish and Vegetable Soup, 69
  Pesto-Vegetable Soup, 85
  Pork and Hominy Stew, 10
  Sausage and Vegetable Soup, 9
  Shrimp and Greens Soup, 25
  Spicy Caramelized Onion Soup, 51
  Tomato-Basil Soup, 70
  Southern Ham Chowder, 78
  Vegetable Cheese Chowder, 79
White Bean and Pasta Soup, 66

wild rice
  Turkey and Wild Rice Chowder, 82
  Wild Rice, Barley, and Mushroom Soup, 16
Yucatan Soup with Lime, 34

tips
Bisques, 78
Broths, the best, 12
Broths, vegetable, 29
Chicken, cooked, 26
Chile peppers, handling, 75
Chowders, 78
Convenience foods, 69
Fish, selecting, 92
Garnishing, 38
Jicama, 22
Mushrooms, storing, 16
Mushrooms, types of, 56
Papayas, 68
Rice, cooking extra, 82
Rice vinegar, 54
Saffron, 11
Salmon, smoked, 50
Shrimp, selecting, 42, 92
Thawing seafood, meats, and poultry, 73
Wine, adding to soup, 46

METRIC COOKING HINTS

By making a few conversions, cooks in Australia, Canada, and the United Kingdom can use the recipes in *Better Homes and Gardens® Fresh and Simple™ Quick-Simmering Soups* with confidence. The charts on this page provide a guide for converting measurements from the U.S. customary system, which is used throughout this book, to the imperial and metric systems. There also is a conversion table for oven temperatures to accommodate the differences in oven calibrations.

Product Differences: Most of the ingredients called for in the recipes in this book are available in English-speaking countries. However, some are known by different names. Here are some common American ingredients and their possible counterparts:

- Sugar is granulated or castor sugar.
- Powdered sugar is icing sugar.
- All-purpose flour is plain household flour or white flour. When self-rising flour is used in place of all-purpose flour in a recipe that calls for leavening, omit the leavening agent (baking soda or baking powder) and salt.
- Light-colored corn syrup is golden syrup.
- Cornstarch is cornflour.
- Baking soda is bicarbonate of soda.
- Vanilla is vanilla essence.
- Green, red, or yellow sweet peppers are capsicums.
- Golden raisins are sultanas.

Volume and Weight: Americans traditionally use cup measures for liquid and solid ingredients. The chart, above right, shows the approximate imperial and metric equivalents. If you are accustomed to weighing solid ingredients, the following approximate equivalents will be helpful.

- 1 cup butter, castor sugar, or rice = 8 ounces = about 250 grams
- 1 cup flour = 4 ounces = about 125 grams
- 1 cup icing sugar = 5 ounces = about 150 grams

Spoon measures are used for smaller amounts of ingredients. Although the size of the tablespoon varies slightly in different countries, for practical purposes and for recipes in this book, a straight substitution is all that's necessary.

Measurements made using cups or spoons always should be level unless stated otherwise.

Equivalents: U.S. = Australia/U.K.

⅛ teaspoon = 0.5 ml
¼ teaspoon = 1 ml
½ teaspoon = 2 ml
1 teaspoon = 5 ml
1 tablespoon = 1 tablespoon
¼ cup = 2 tablespoons = 2 fluid ounces = 60 ml
⅓ cup = ¼ cup = 3 fluid ounces = 90 ml
½ cup = ⅓ cup = 4 fluid ounces = 120 ml
⅔ cup = ½ cup = 5 fluid ounces = 150 ml
¾ cup = ⅔ cup = 6 fluid ounces = 180 ml
1 cup = ¾ cup = 8 fluid ounces = 240 ml
1¼ cups = 1 cup
2 cups = 1 pint
1 quart = 1 liter
½ inch = 1.27 cm
1 inch = 2.54 cm

Baking Pan Sizes

American	Metric
8×1½-inch round baking pan	20×4-cm cake tin
9×1½-inch round baking pan	23×3.5-cm cake tin
11×7×1½-inch baking pan	28×18×4-cm baking tin
13×9×2-inch baking pan	30×20×3-cm baking tin
2-quart rectangular baking dish	30×20×3-cm baking tin
15×10×1-inch baking pan	30×25×2-cm baking tin (Swiss roll tin)
9-inch pie plate	22×4- or 23×4-cm pie plate
7- or 8-inch springform pan	18- or 20-cm springform or loose-bottom cake tin
9×5×3-inch loaf pan	23×13×7-cm or 2-pound narrow loaf tin or pâté tin
1½-quart casserole	1.5-liter casserole
2-quart casserole	2-liter casserole

Oven Temperature Equivalents

Fahrenheit Setting	Celsius Setting*	Gas Setting
300°F	150°C	Gas Mark 2 (slow)
325°F	160°C	Gas Mark 3 (moderately slow)
350°F	180°C	Gas Mark 4 (moderate)
375°F	190°C	Gas Mark 5 (moderately hot)
400°F	200°C	Gas Mark 6 (hot)
425°F	220°C	Gas Mark 7
450°F	230°C	Gas Mark 8 (very hot)
Broil		Grill

*Electric and gas ovens may be calibrated using Celsius. However, for an electric oven, increase the Celsius setting 10 to 20 degrees when cooking above 160°C. For convection or forced-air ovens (gas or electric), lower the temperature setting 10°C when cooking at all heat levels.